50 inspirational images you can color to inspire yourself and others! Many times in life the best ideas come to us when we least expect it! Use this book to relax and open your creative mind, open spaces have been left for your notes or doodles......have fun!

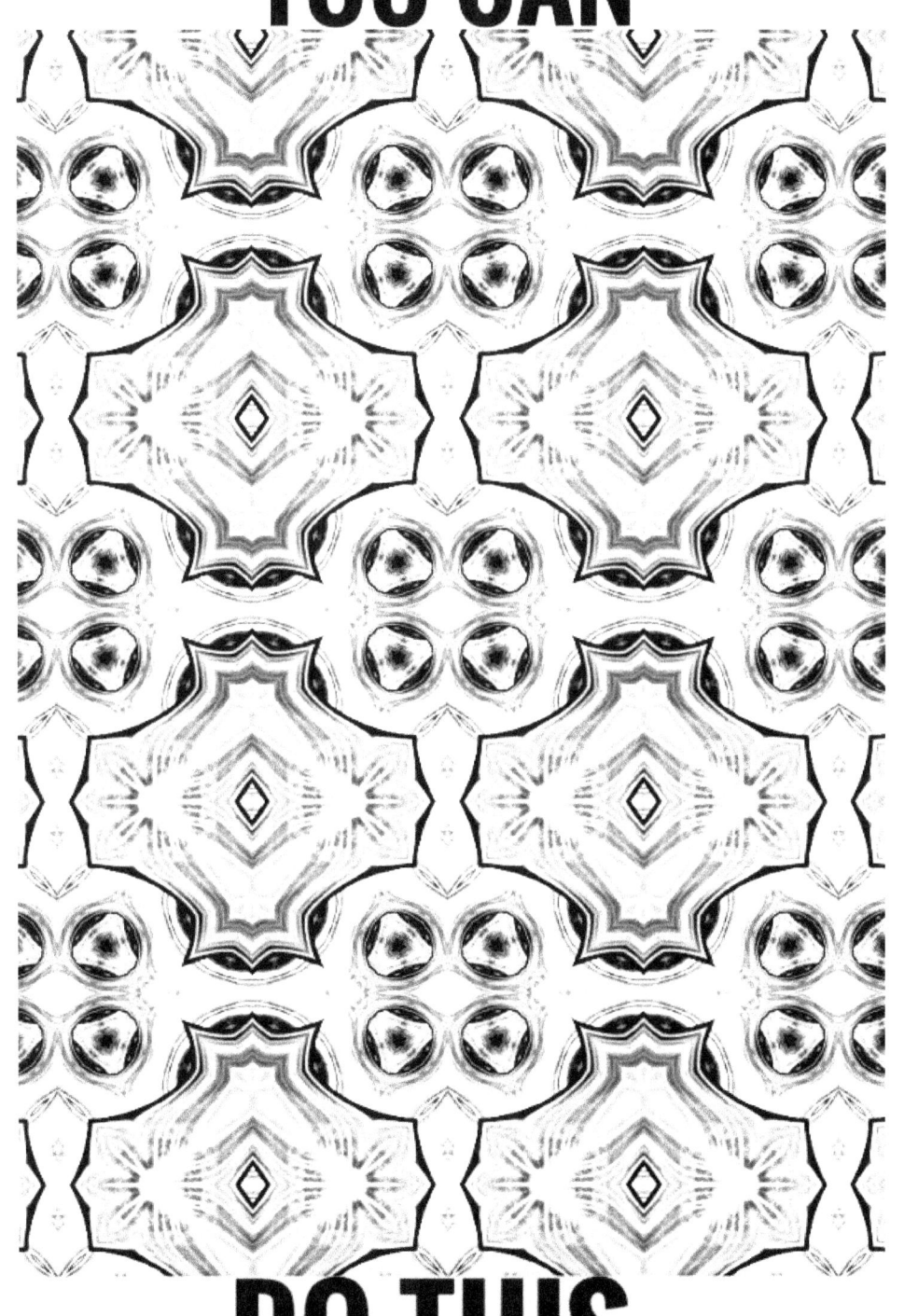

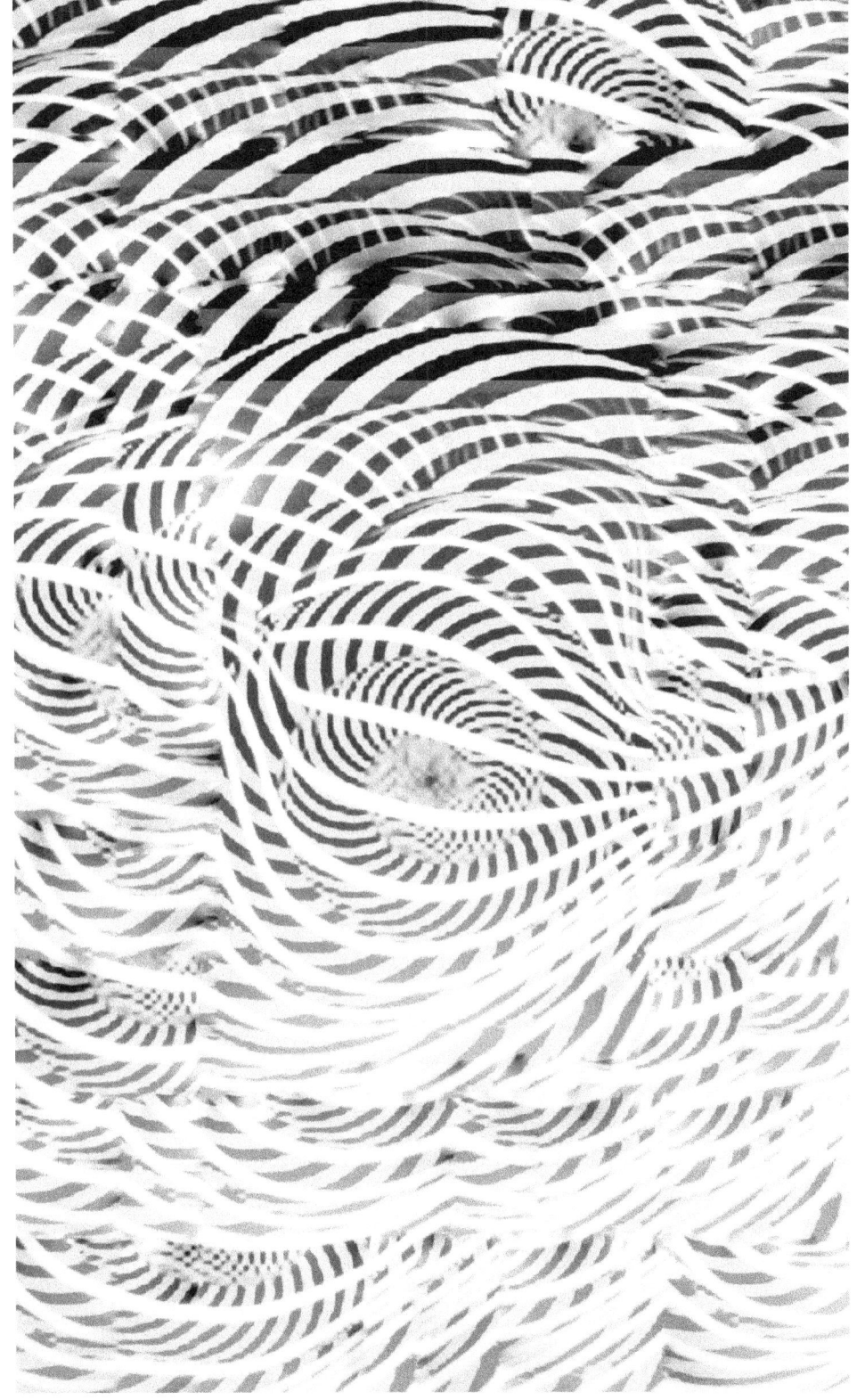

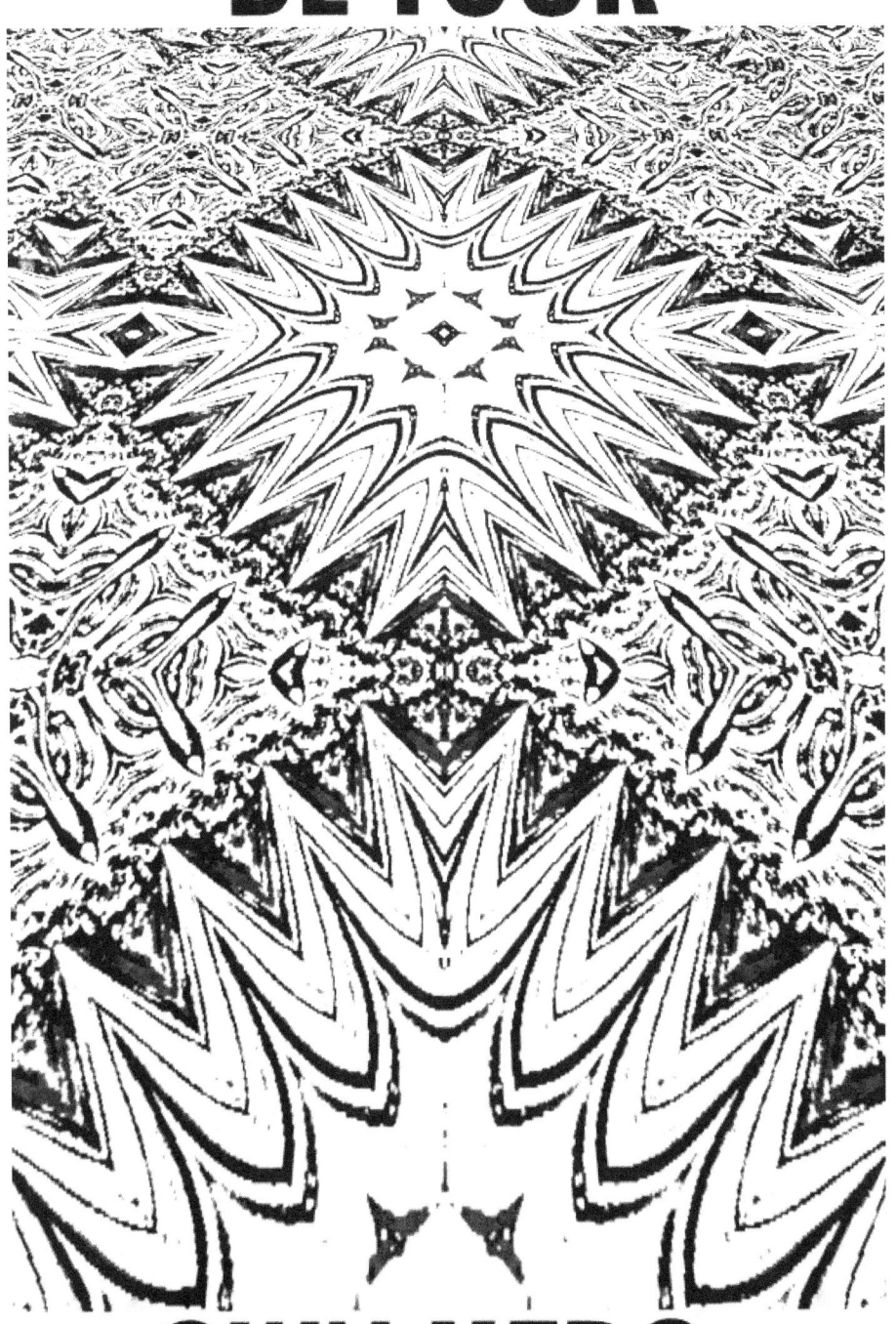

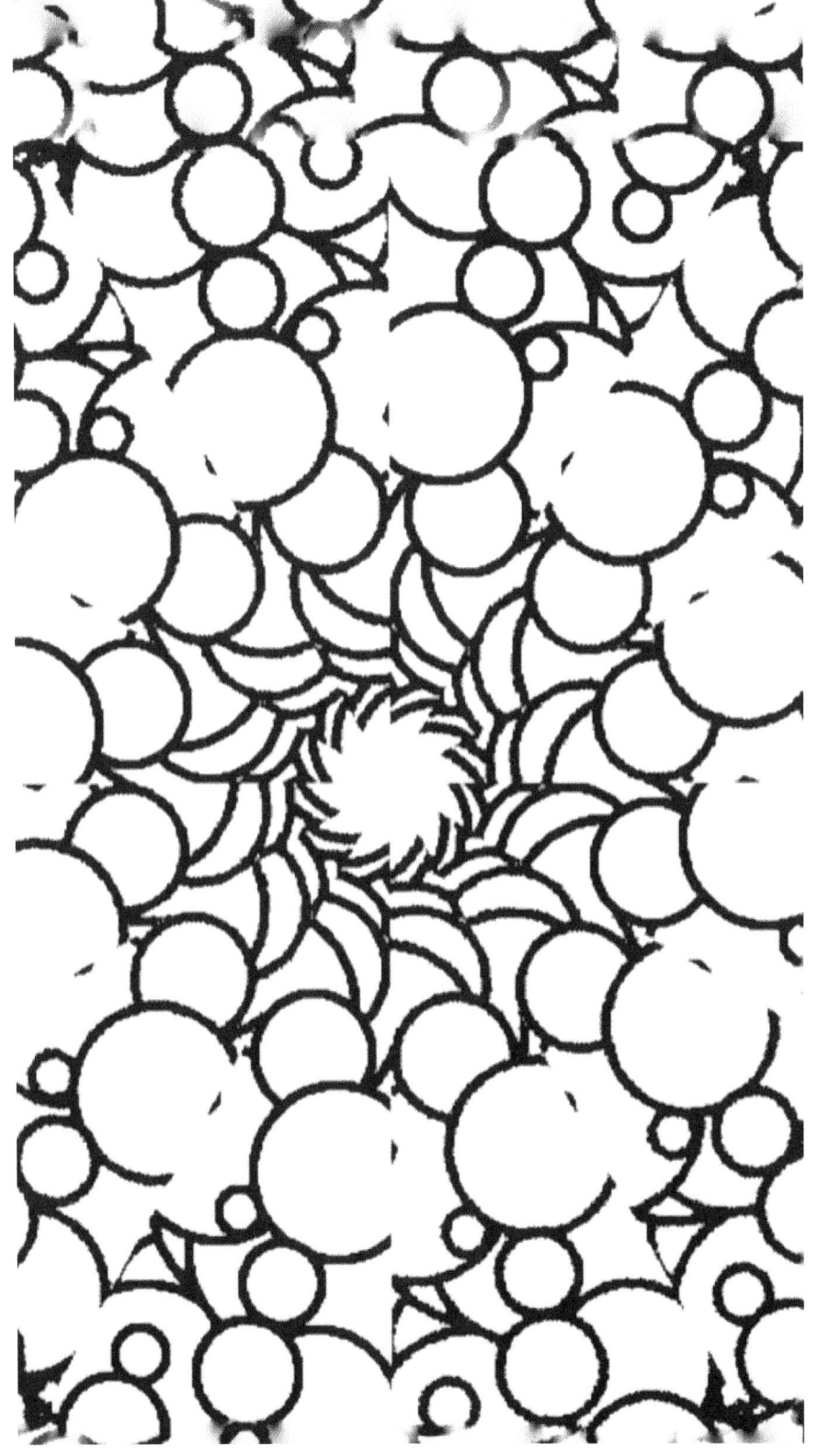

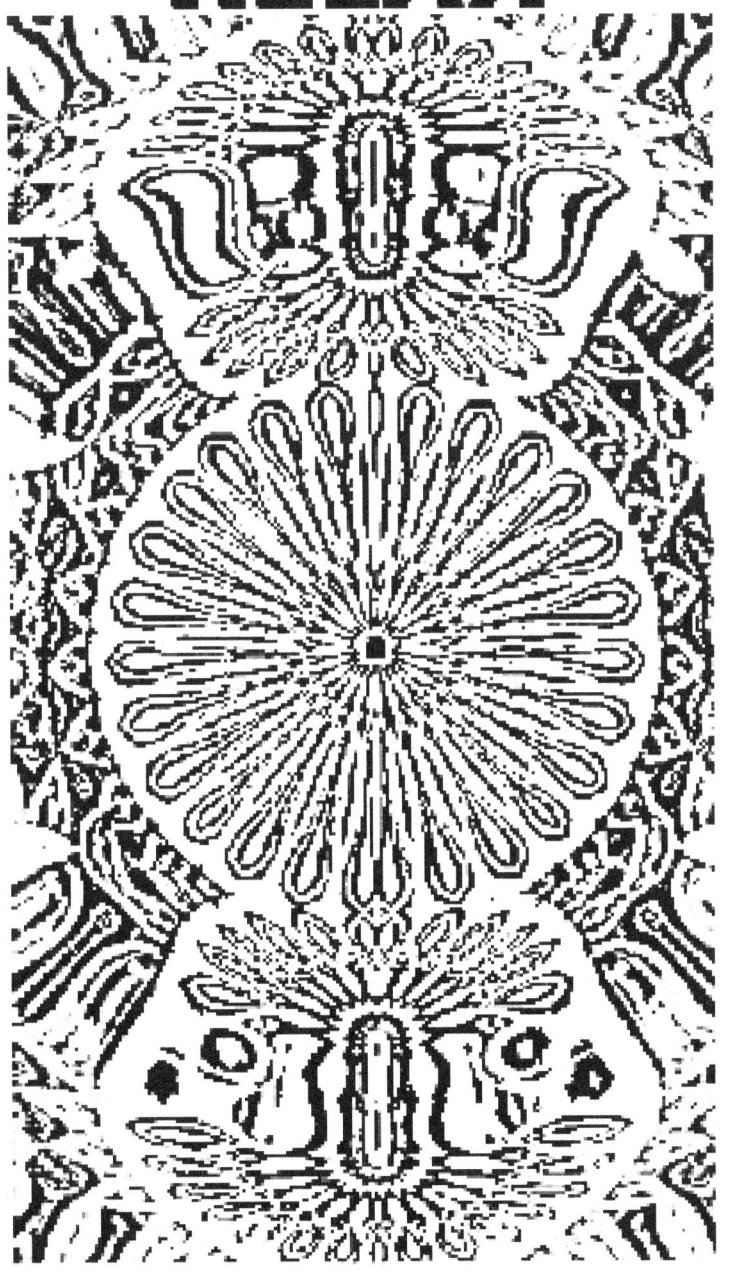

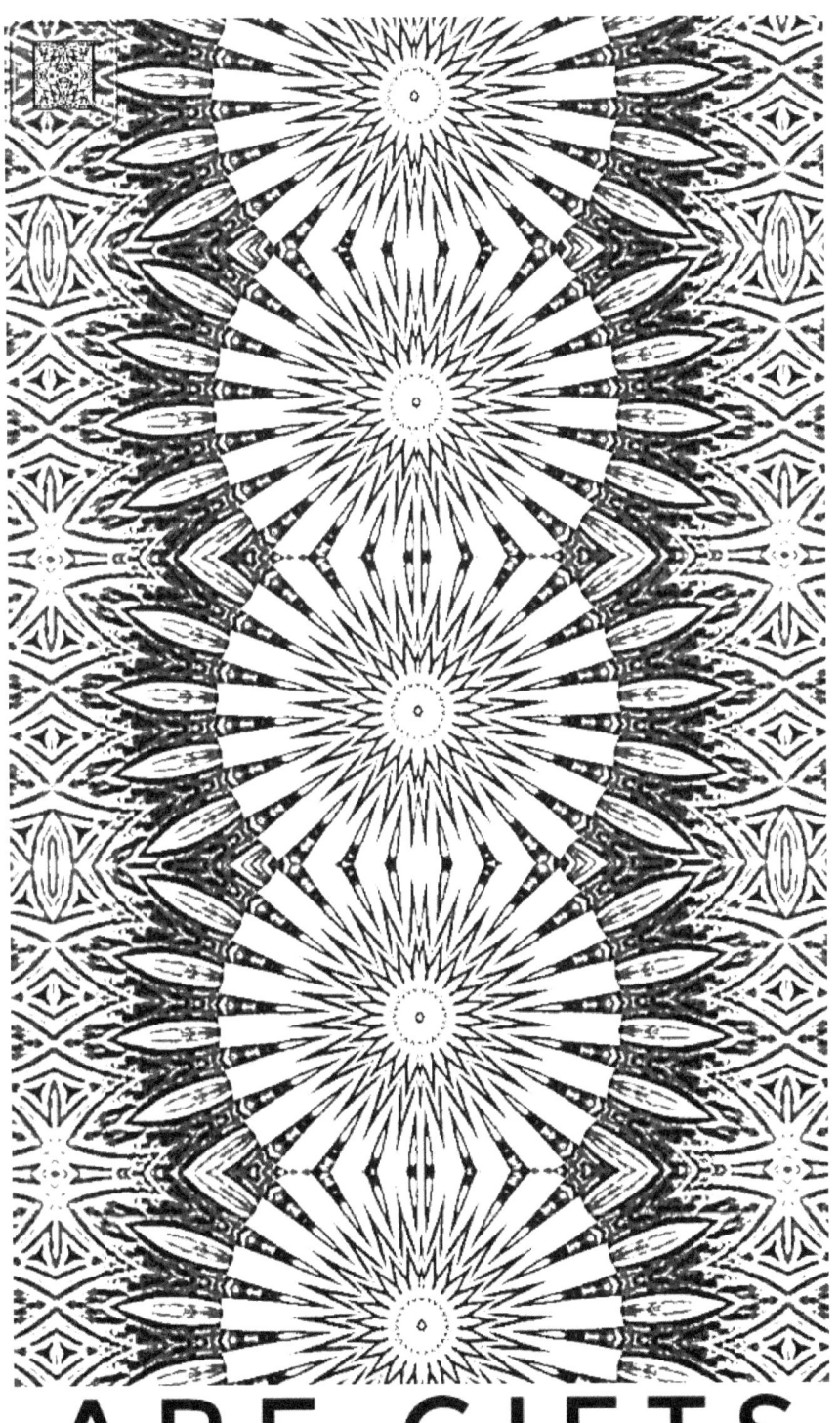

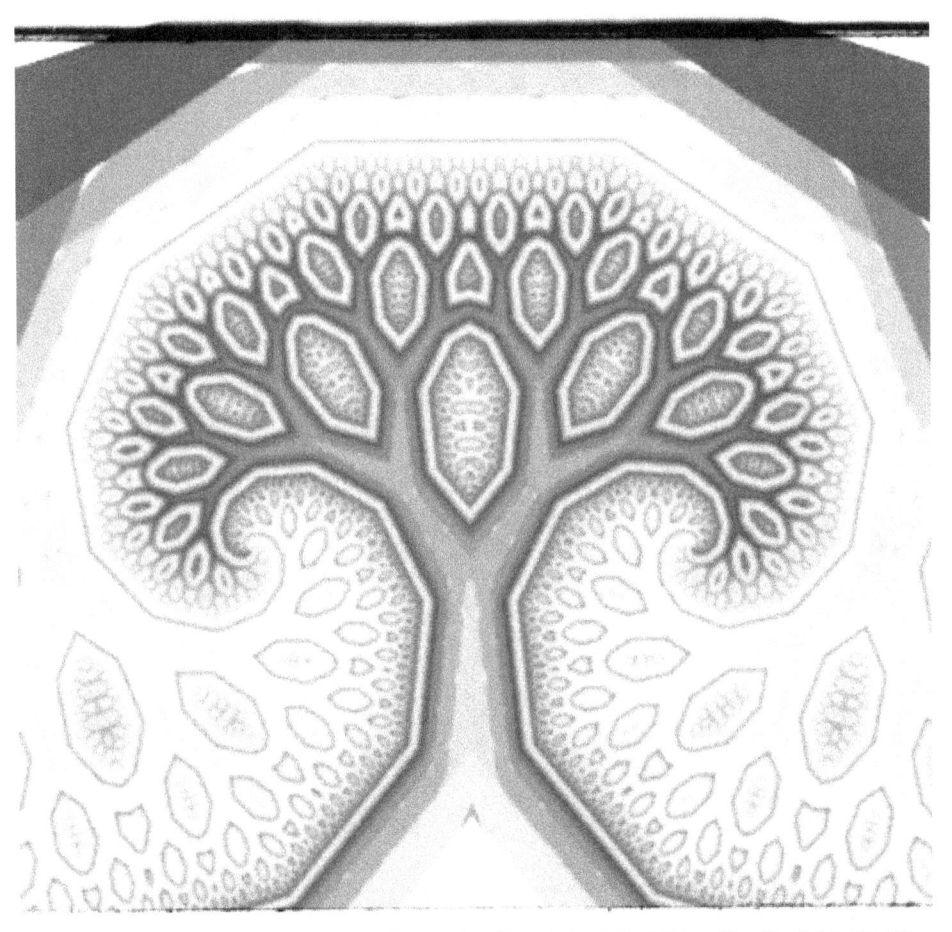

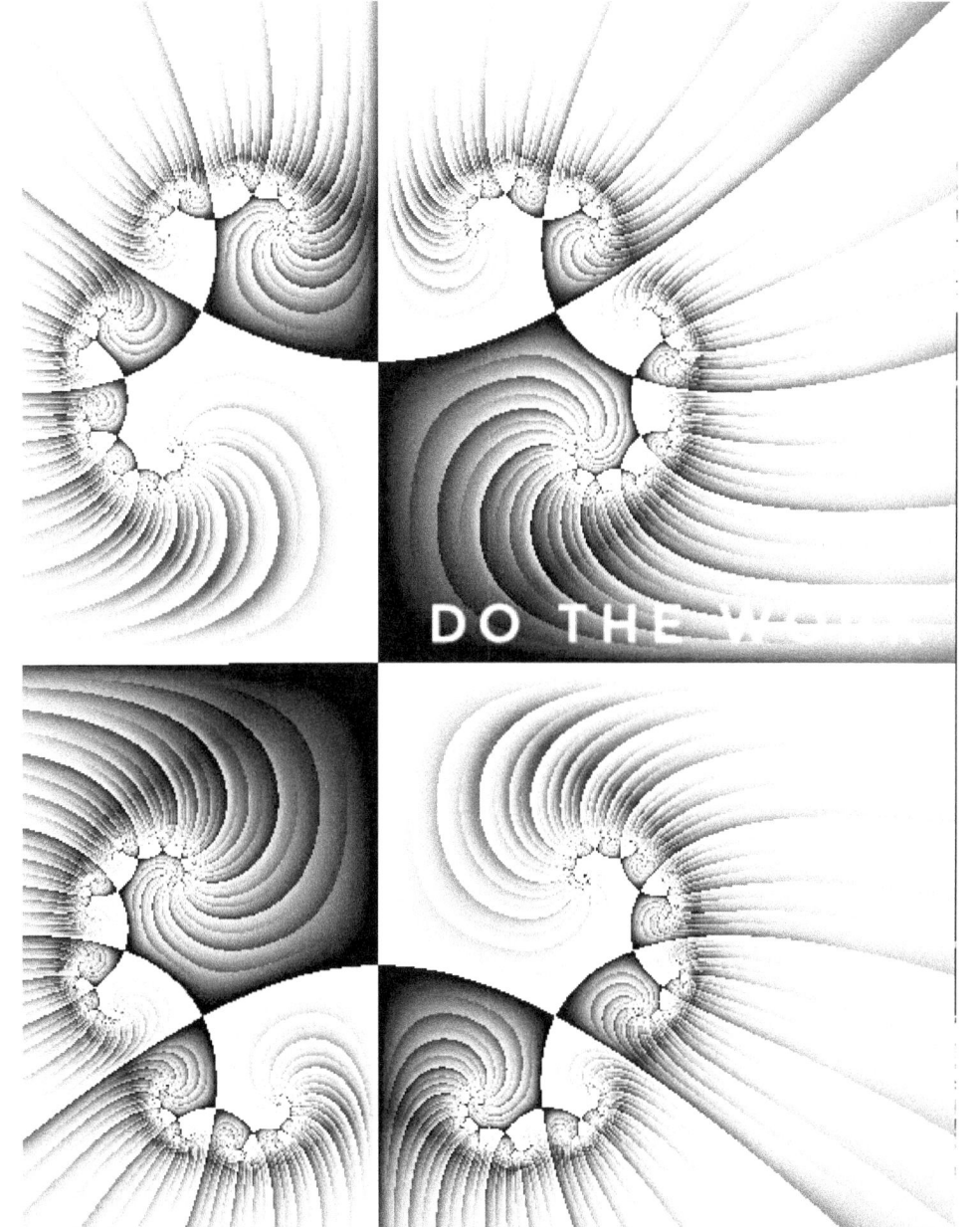

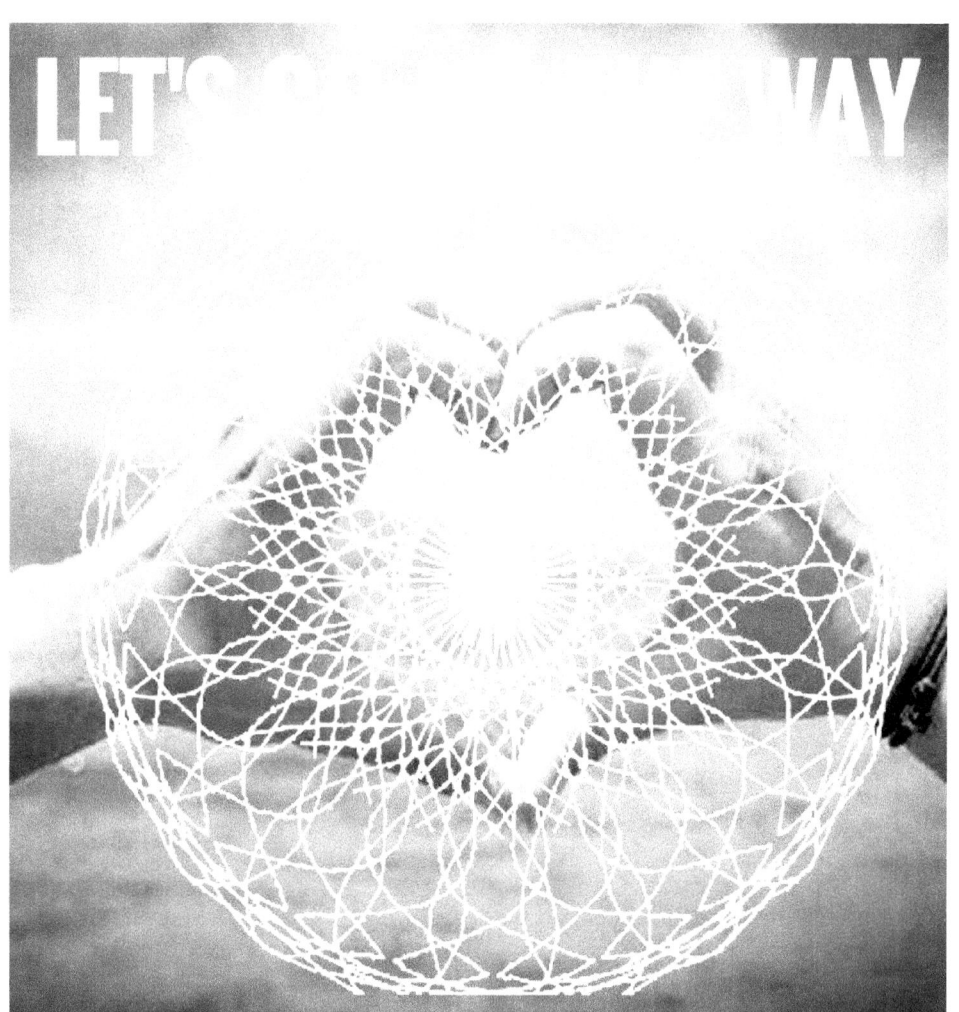

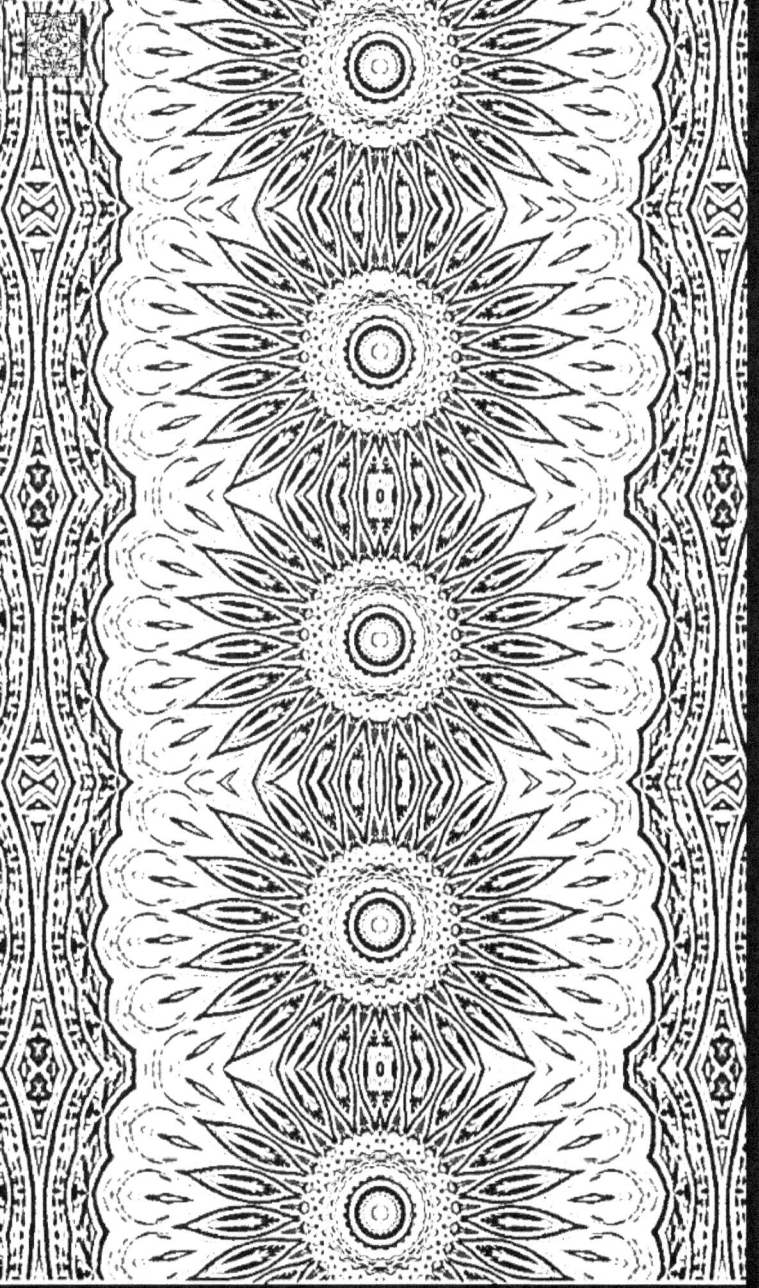

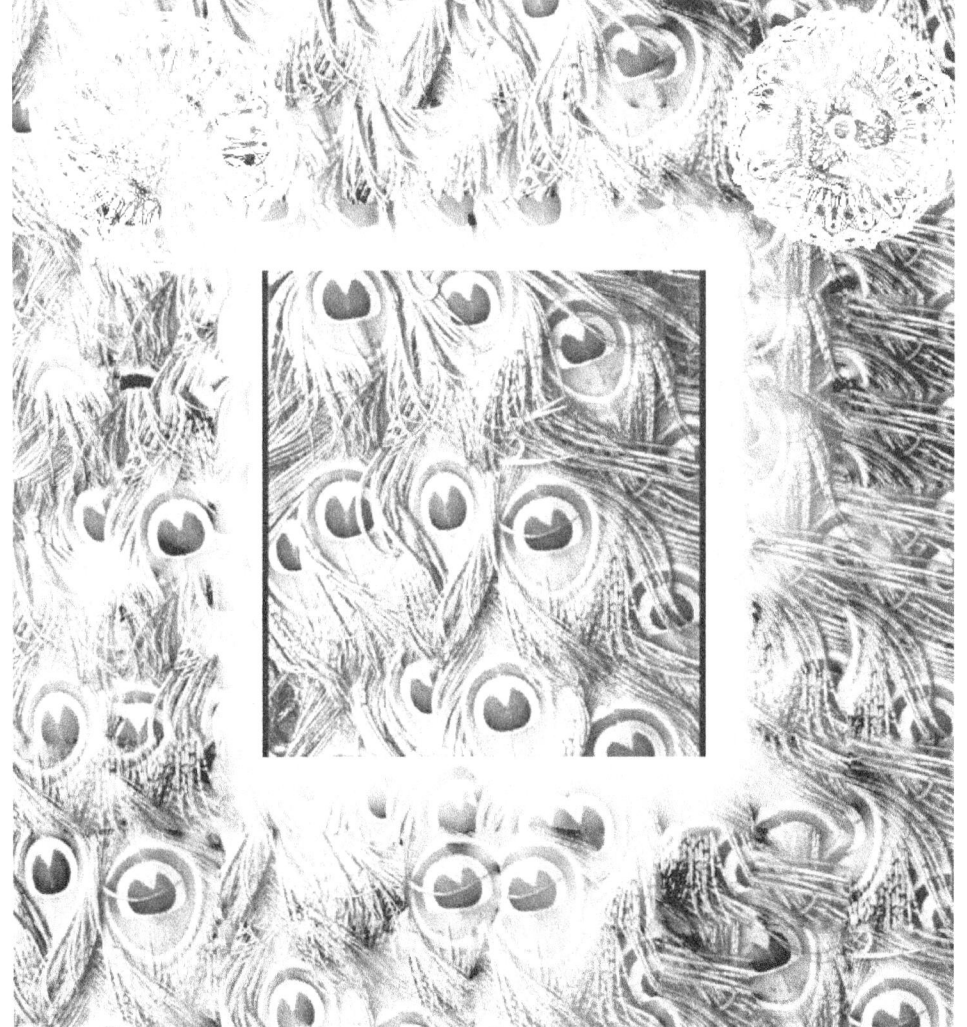

# YOU ARE THE ONE

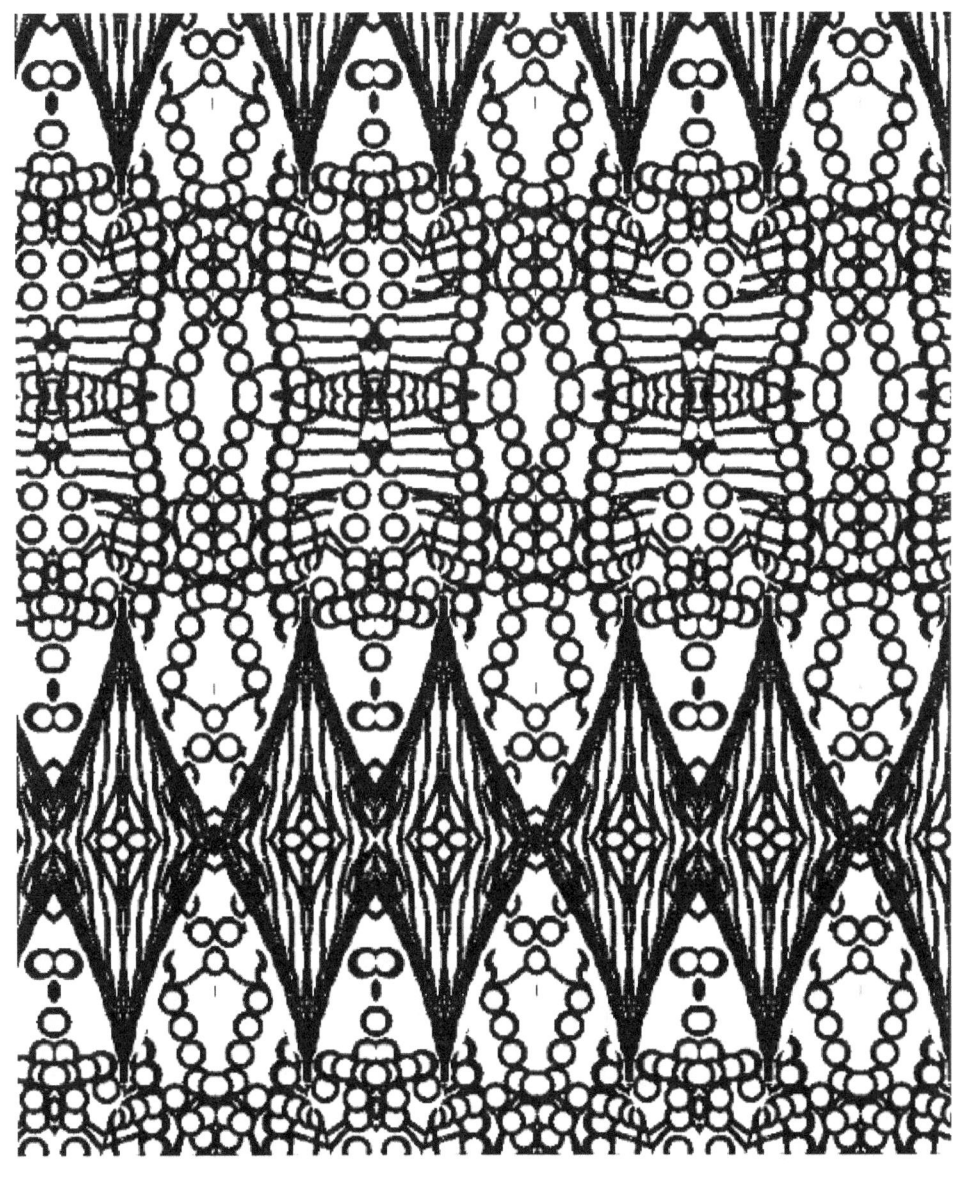

# ALL IS WITHIN YOU

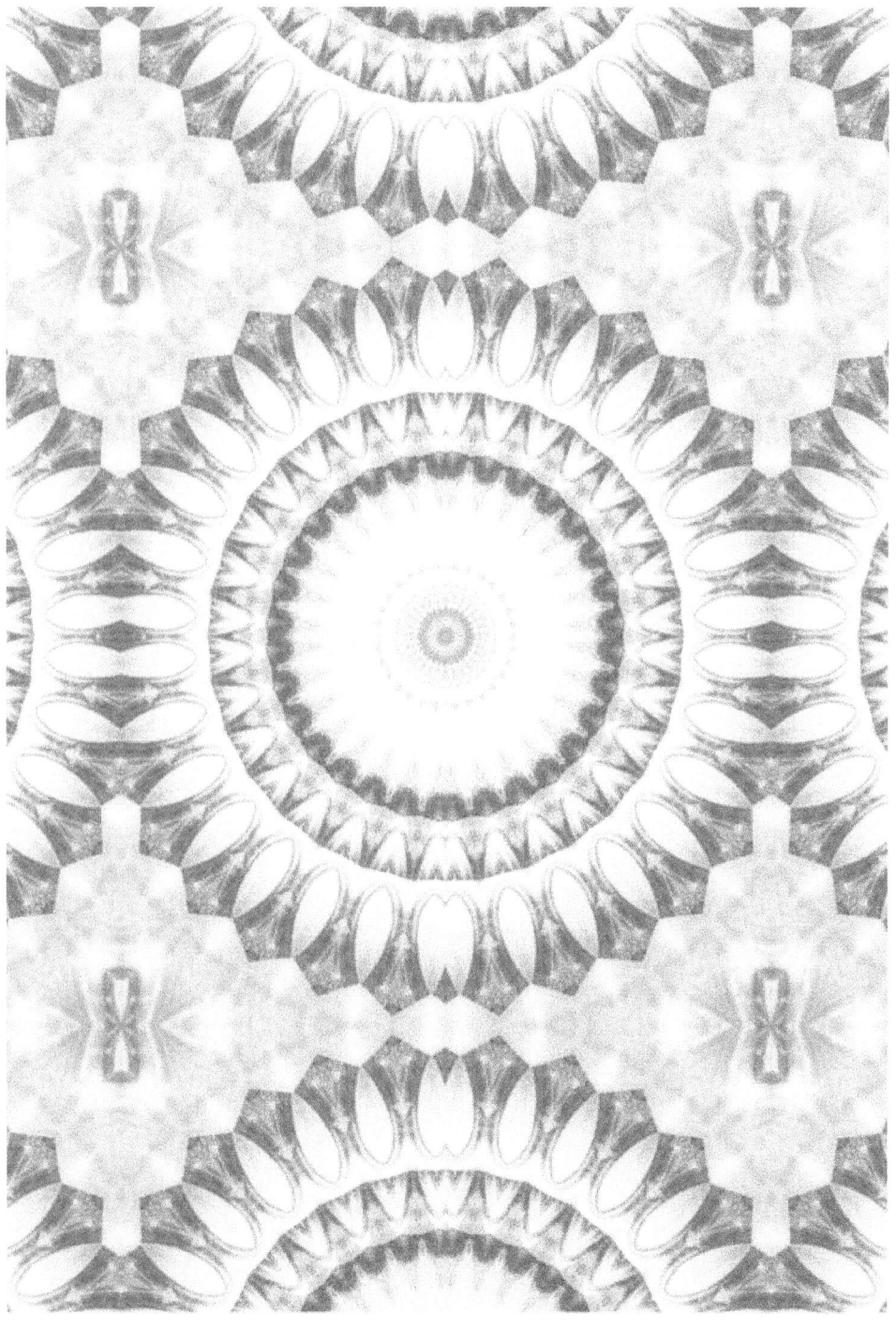

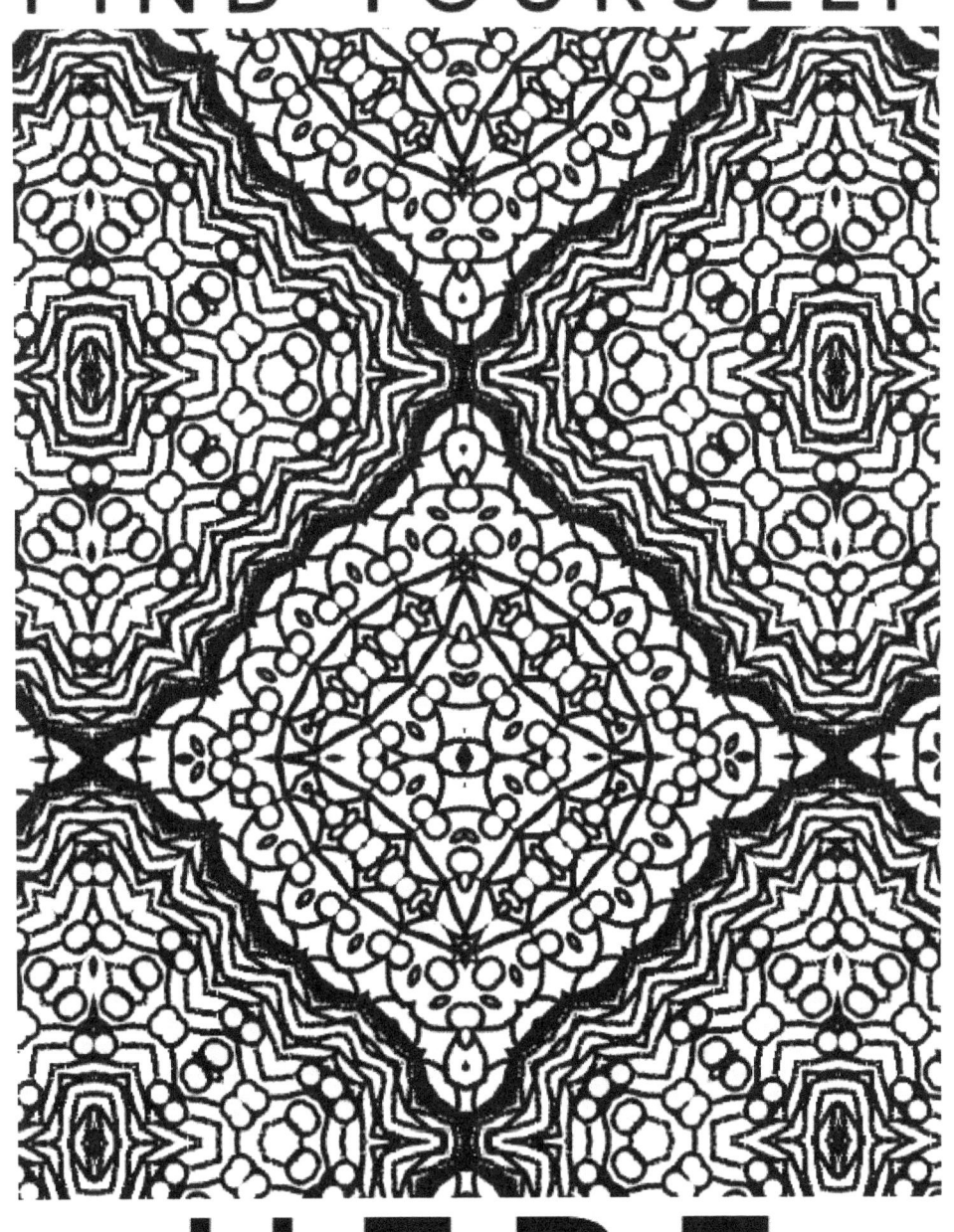

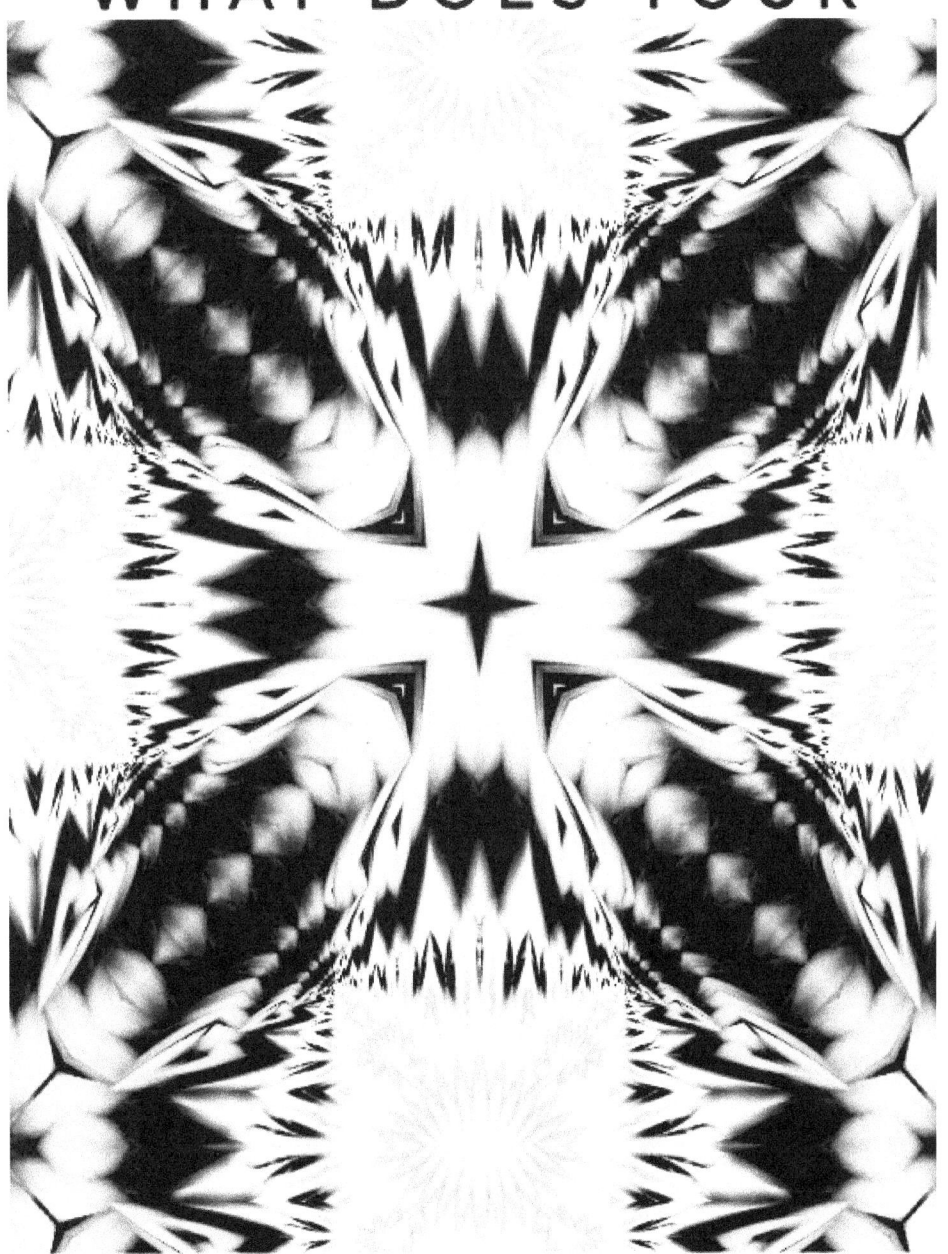

# TAKE

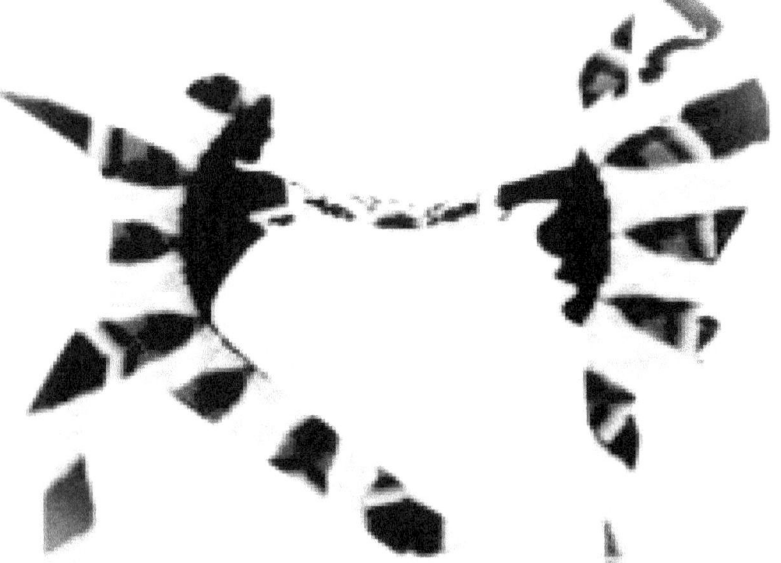

## THE CHANCE

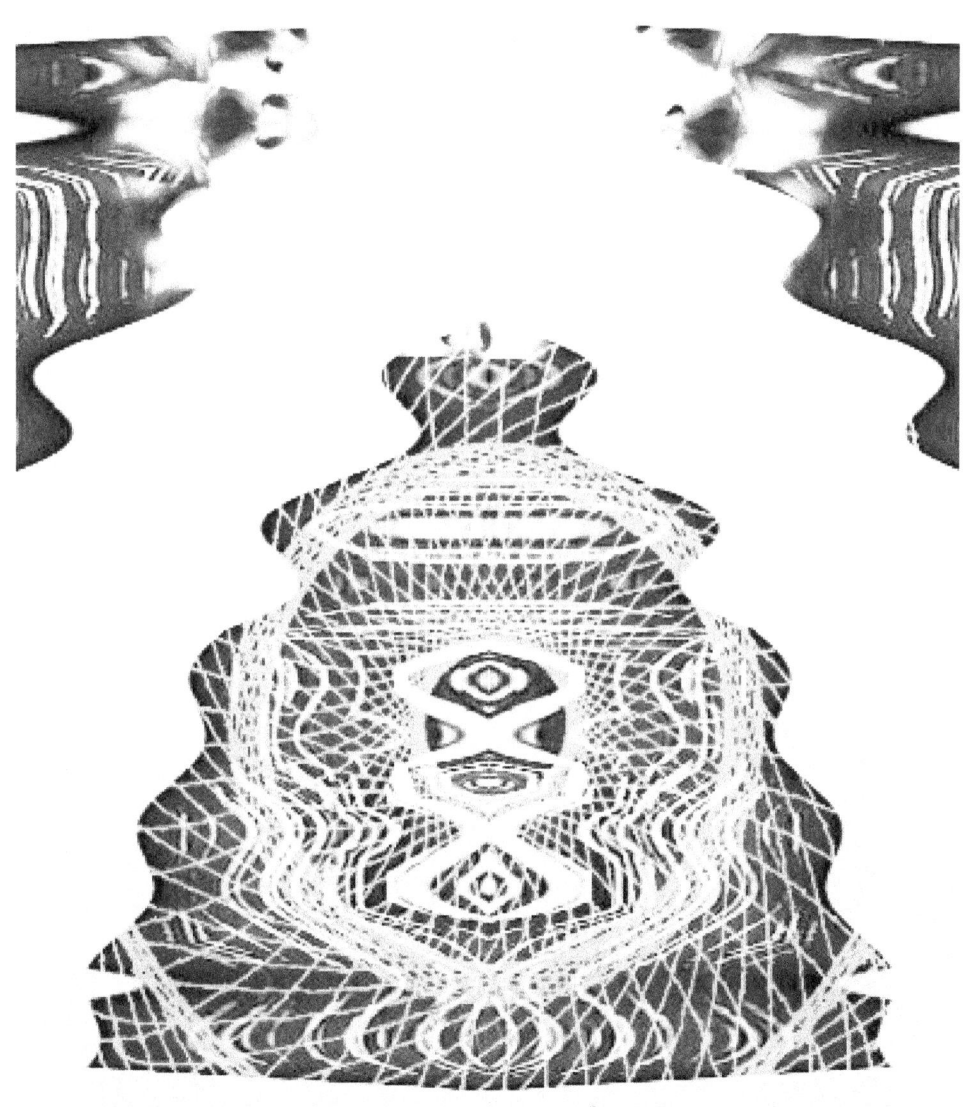

# FOLLOW YOUR HEART

# STAND THE

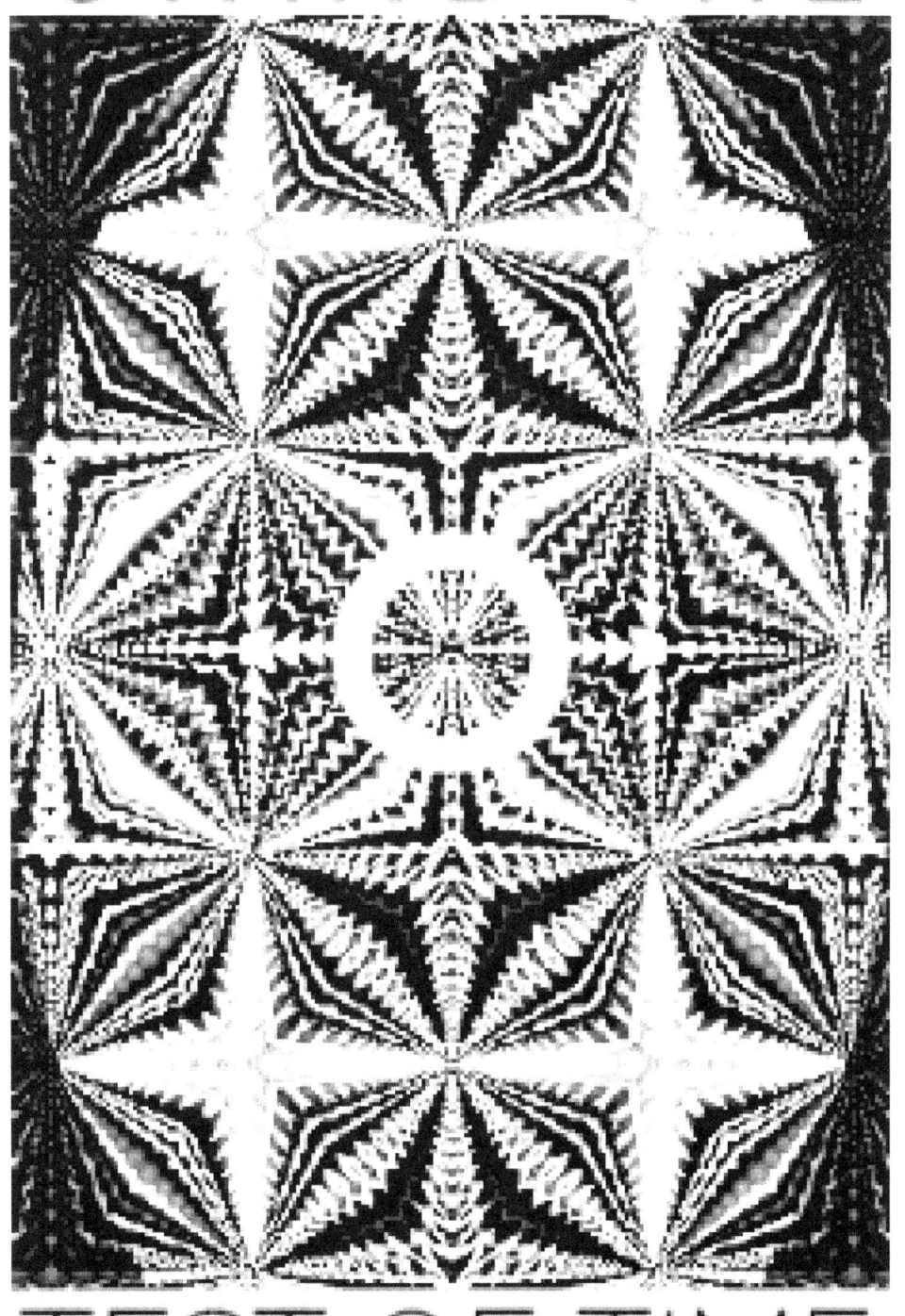

# TEST OF TIME

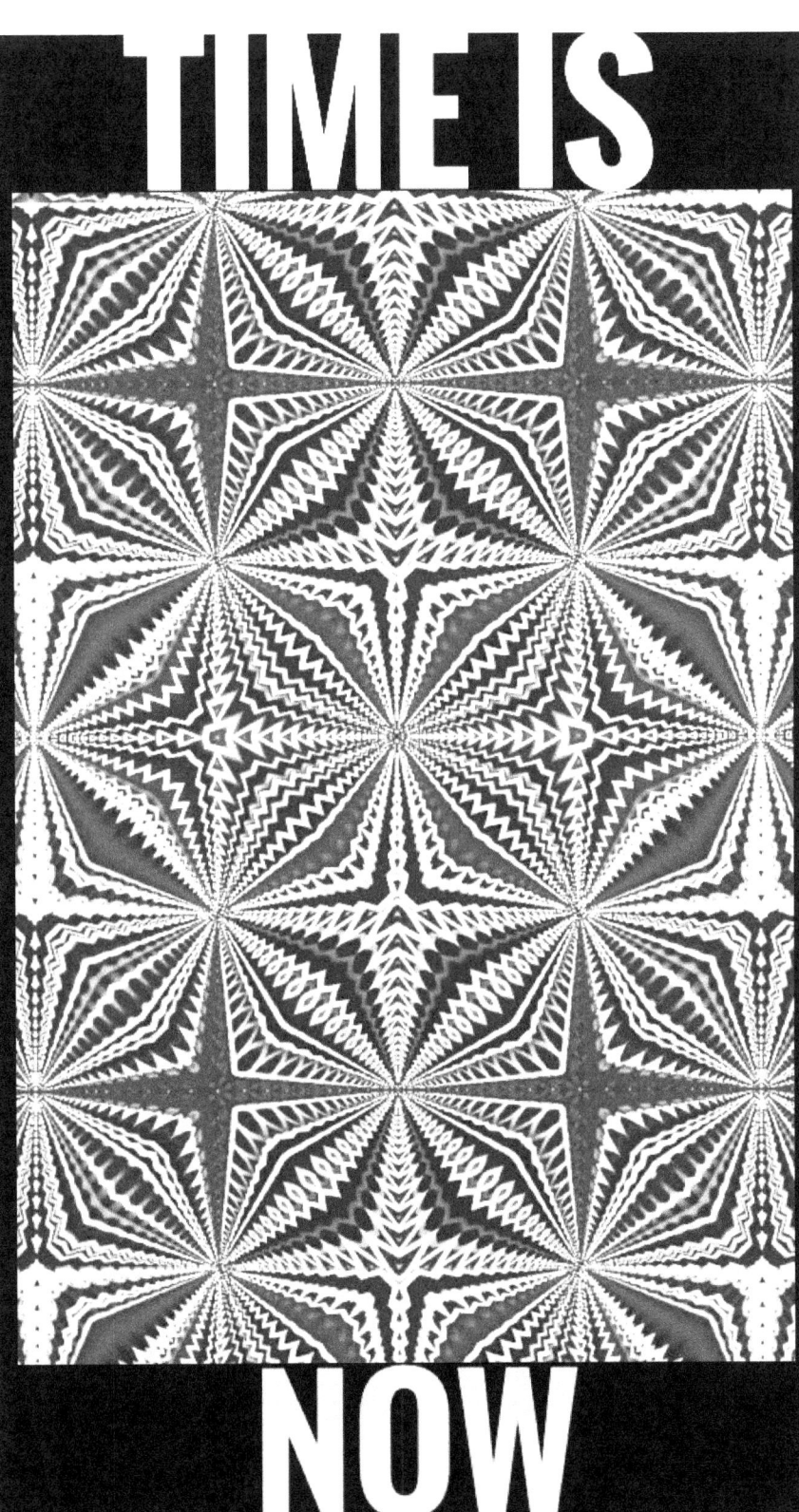

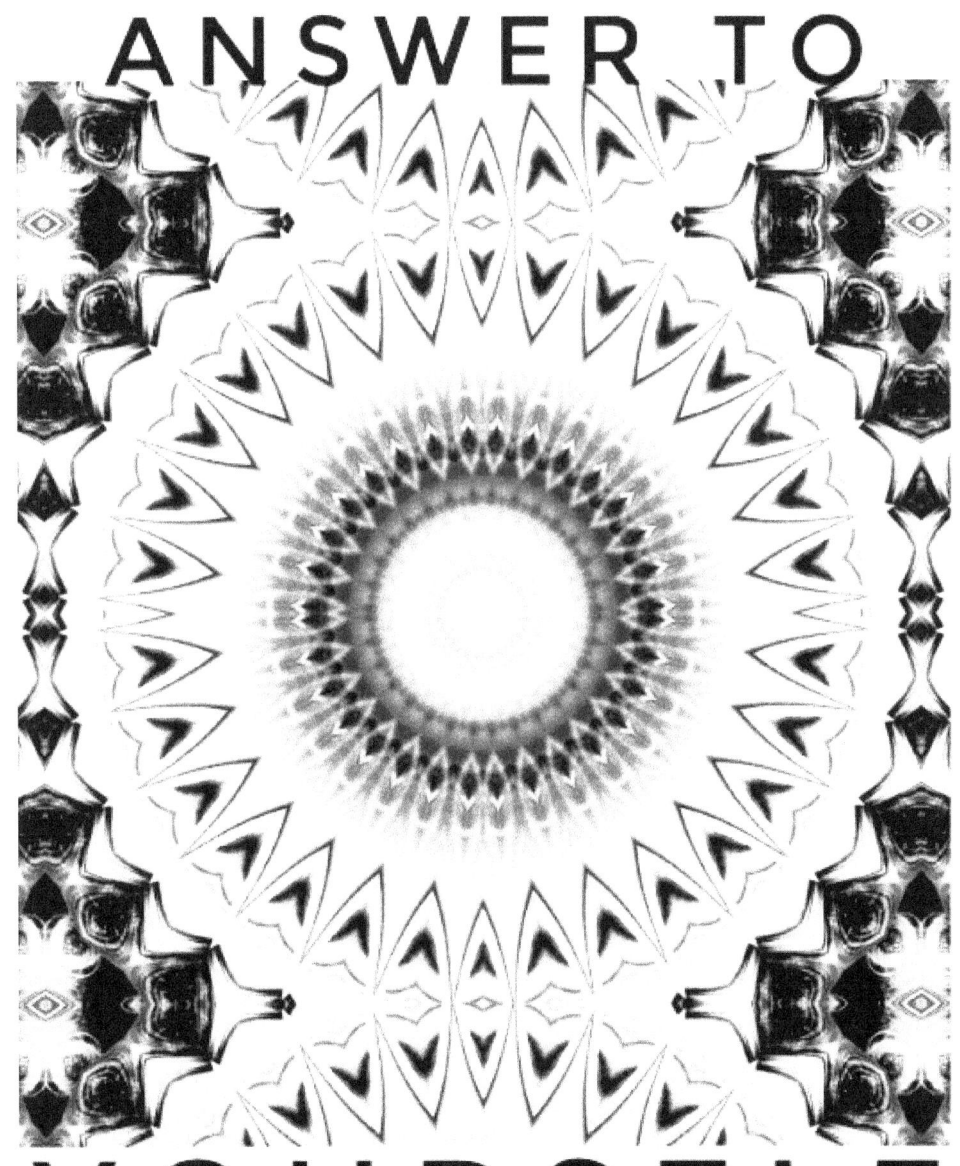

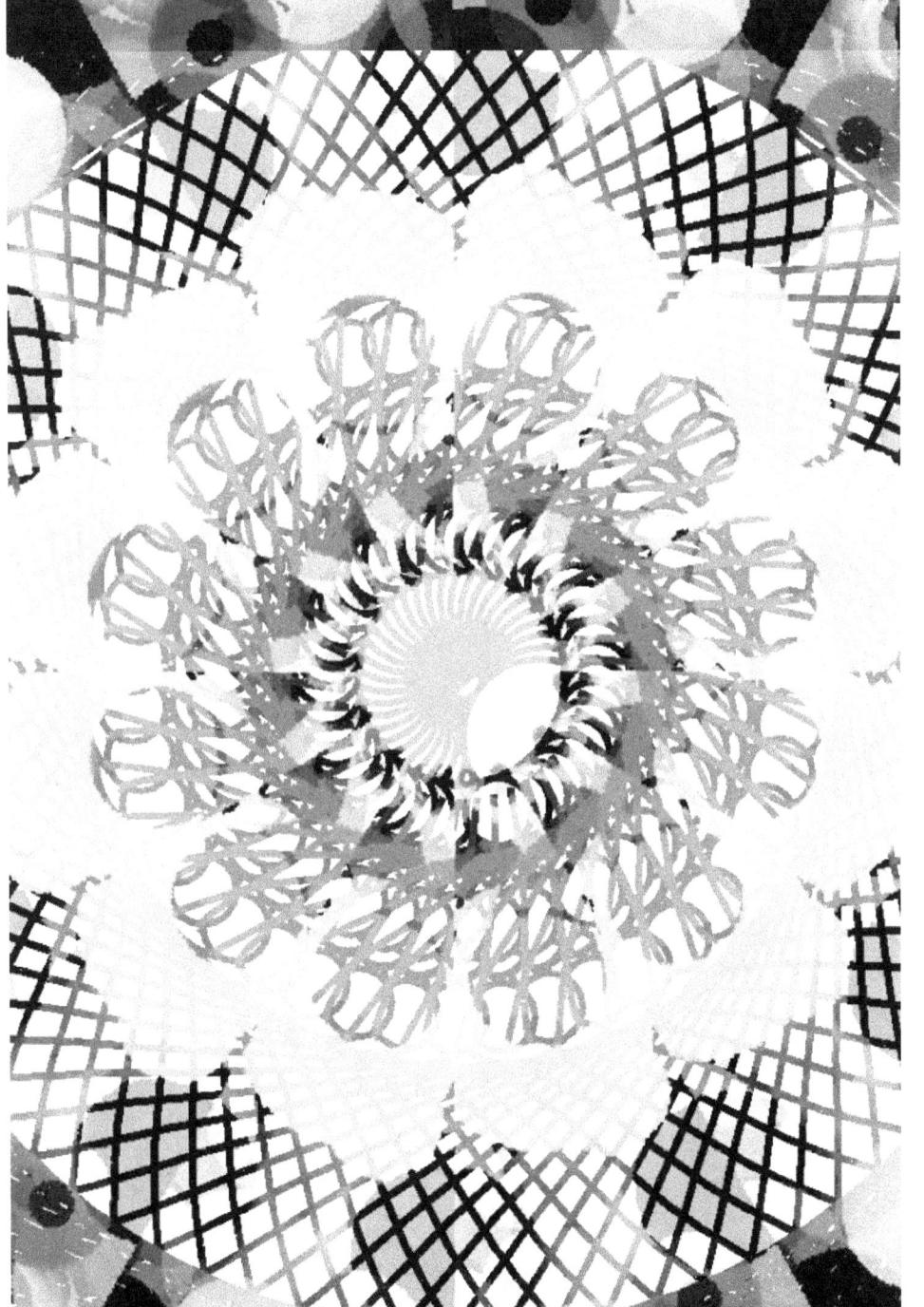

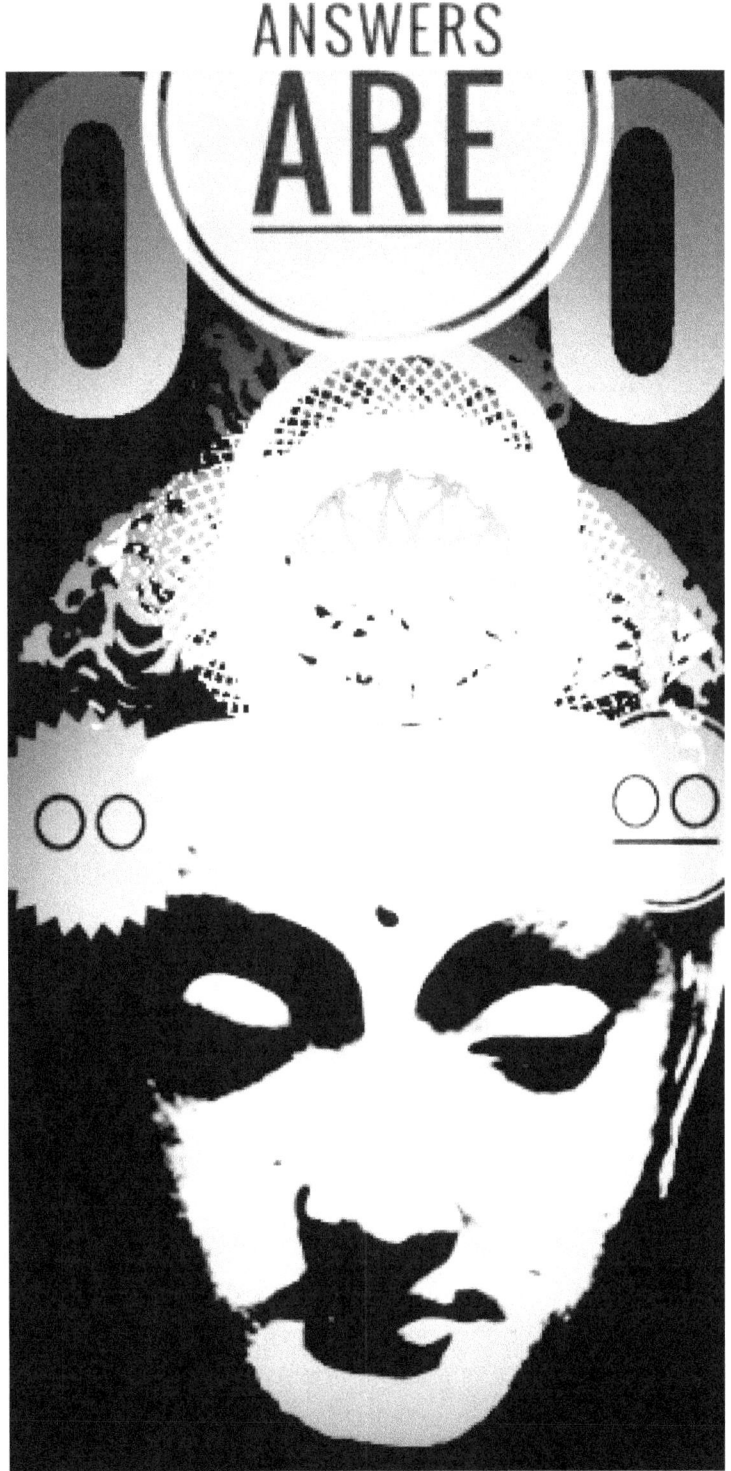

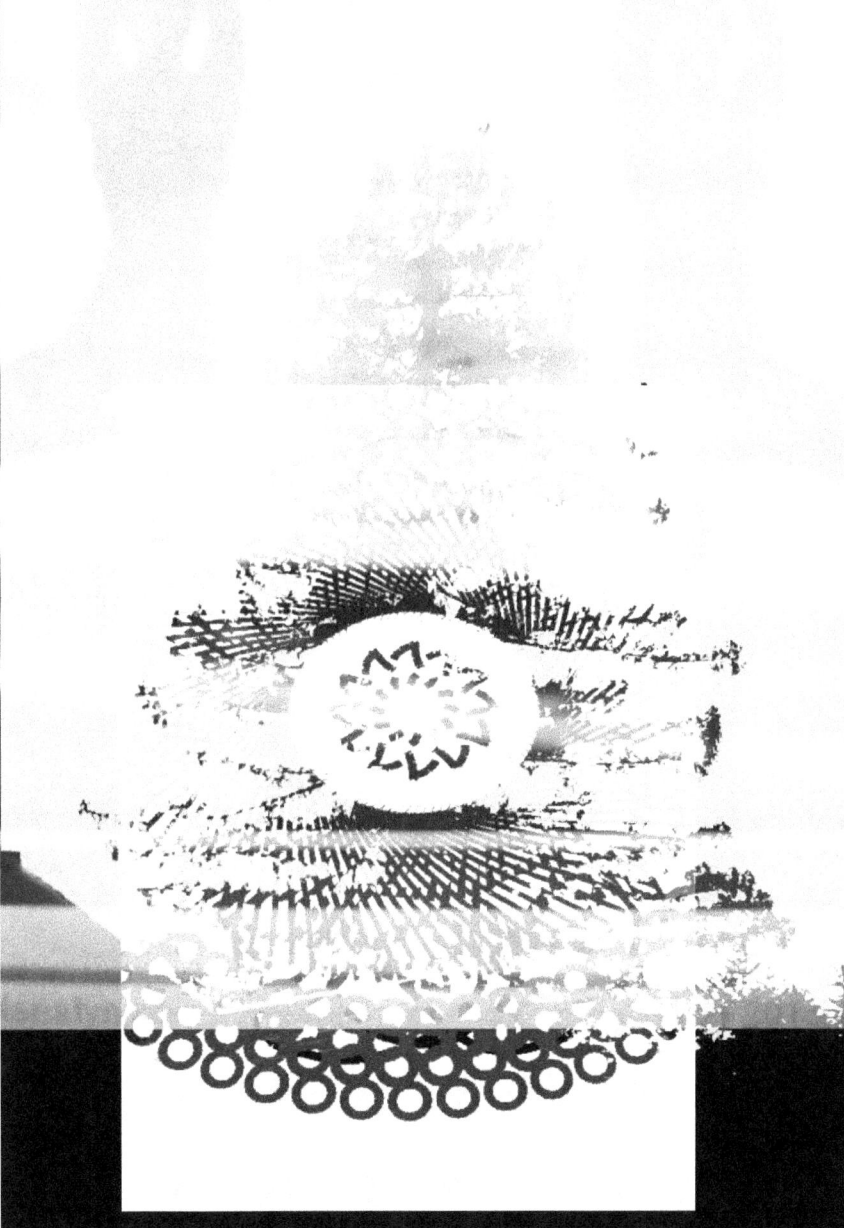

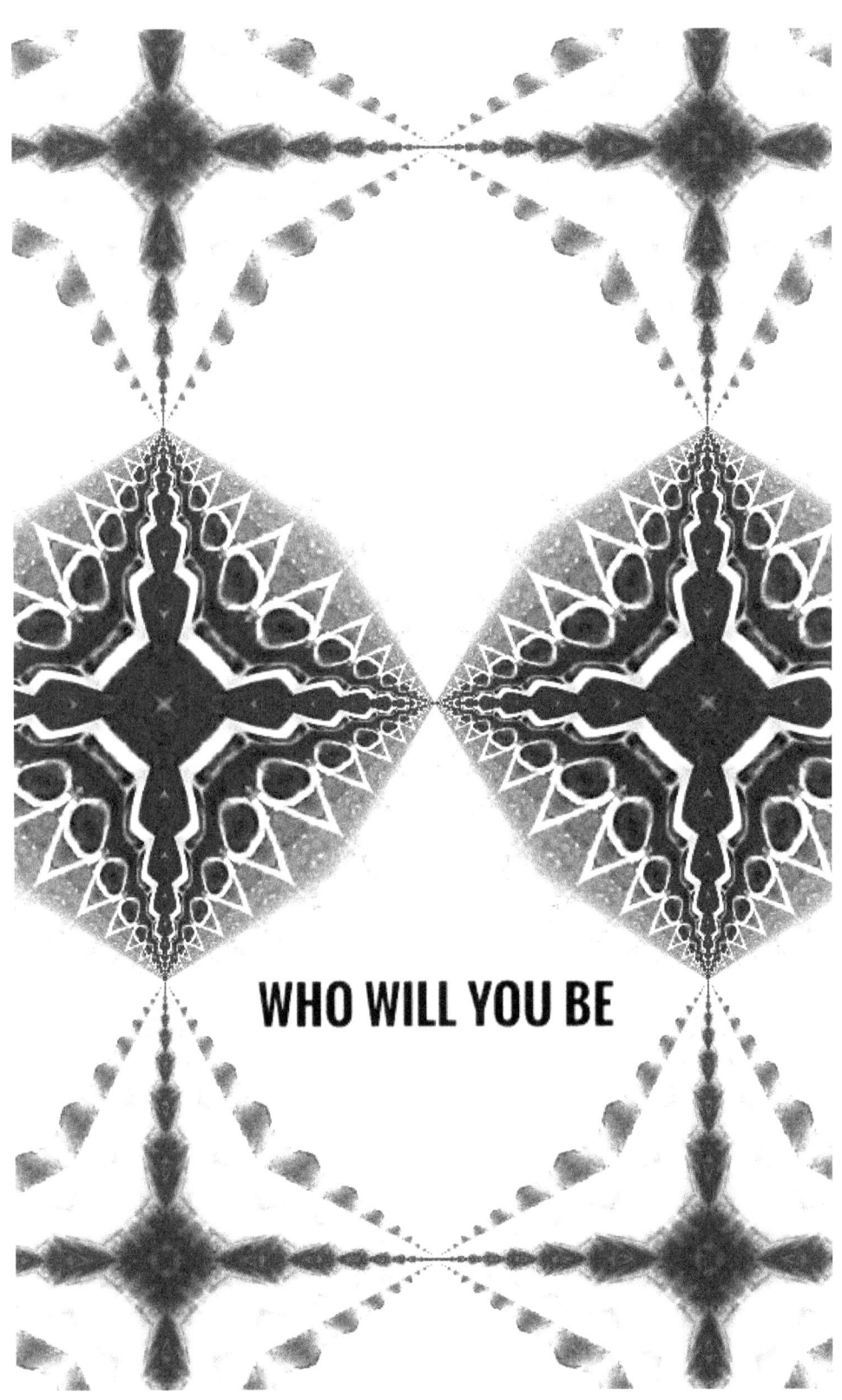

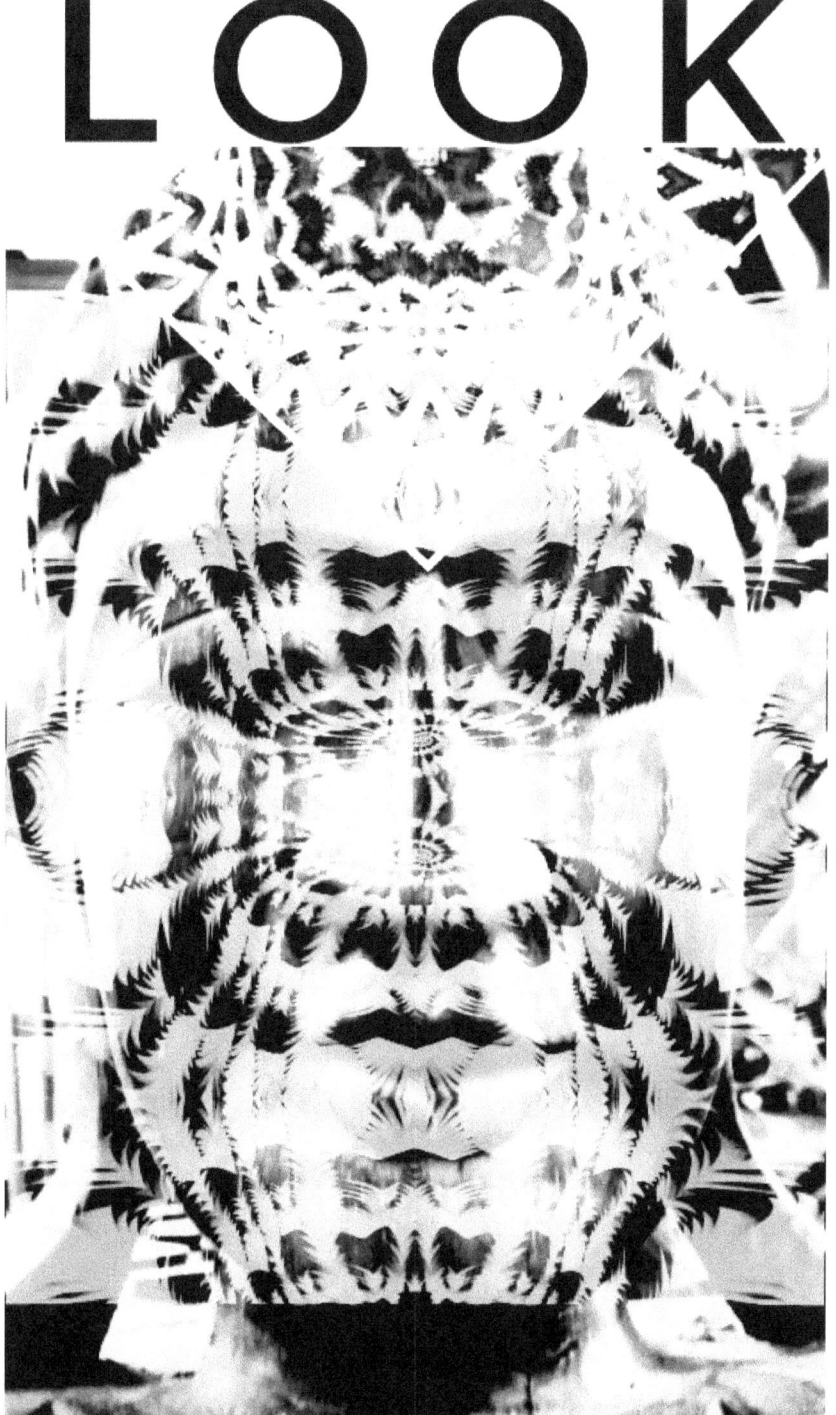

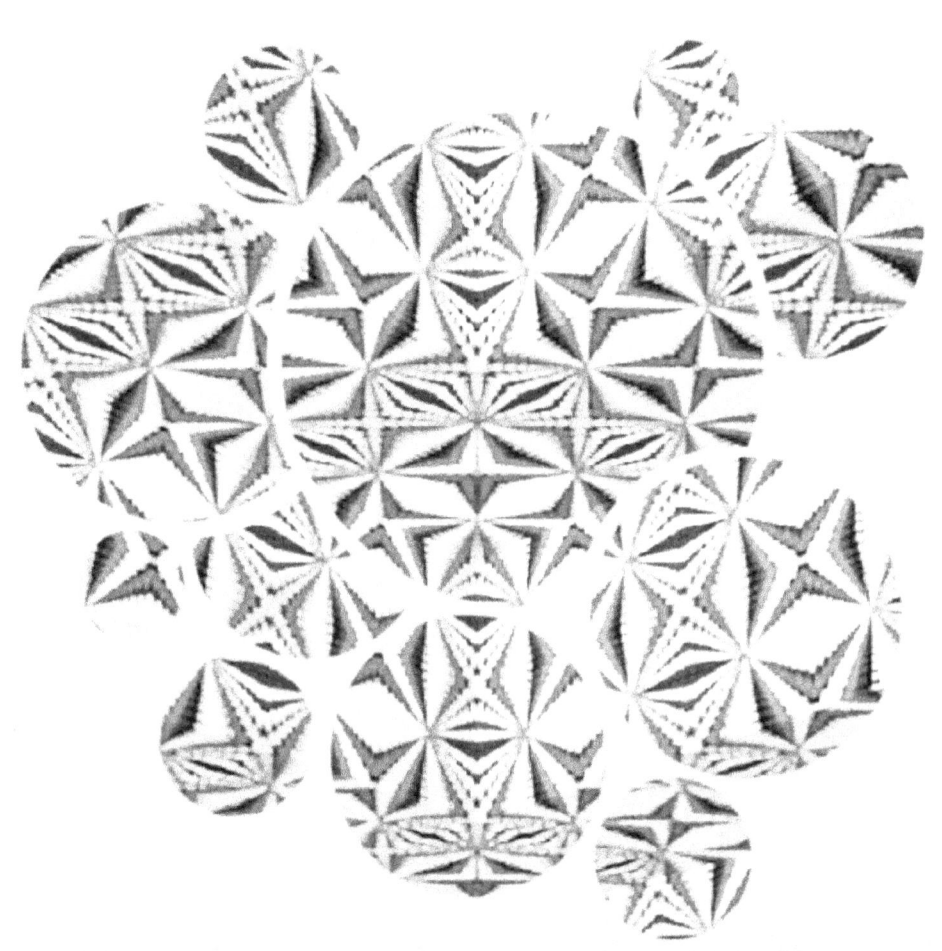

**EVERY MOMENT IS A GIFT THAT'S WHY WE CALL IT THE PRESENT**

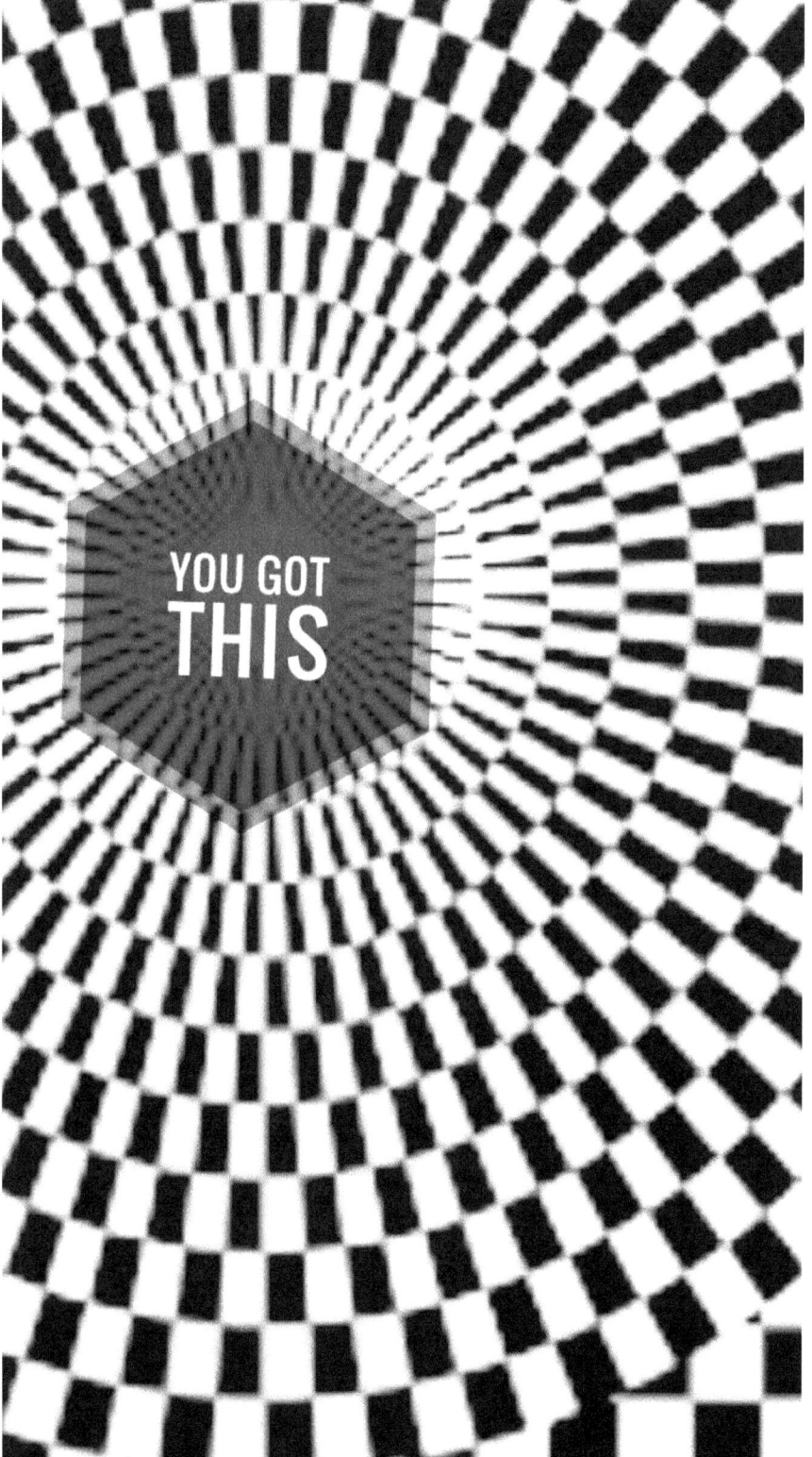

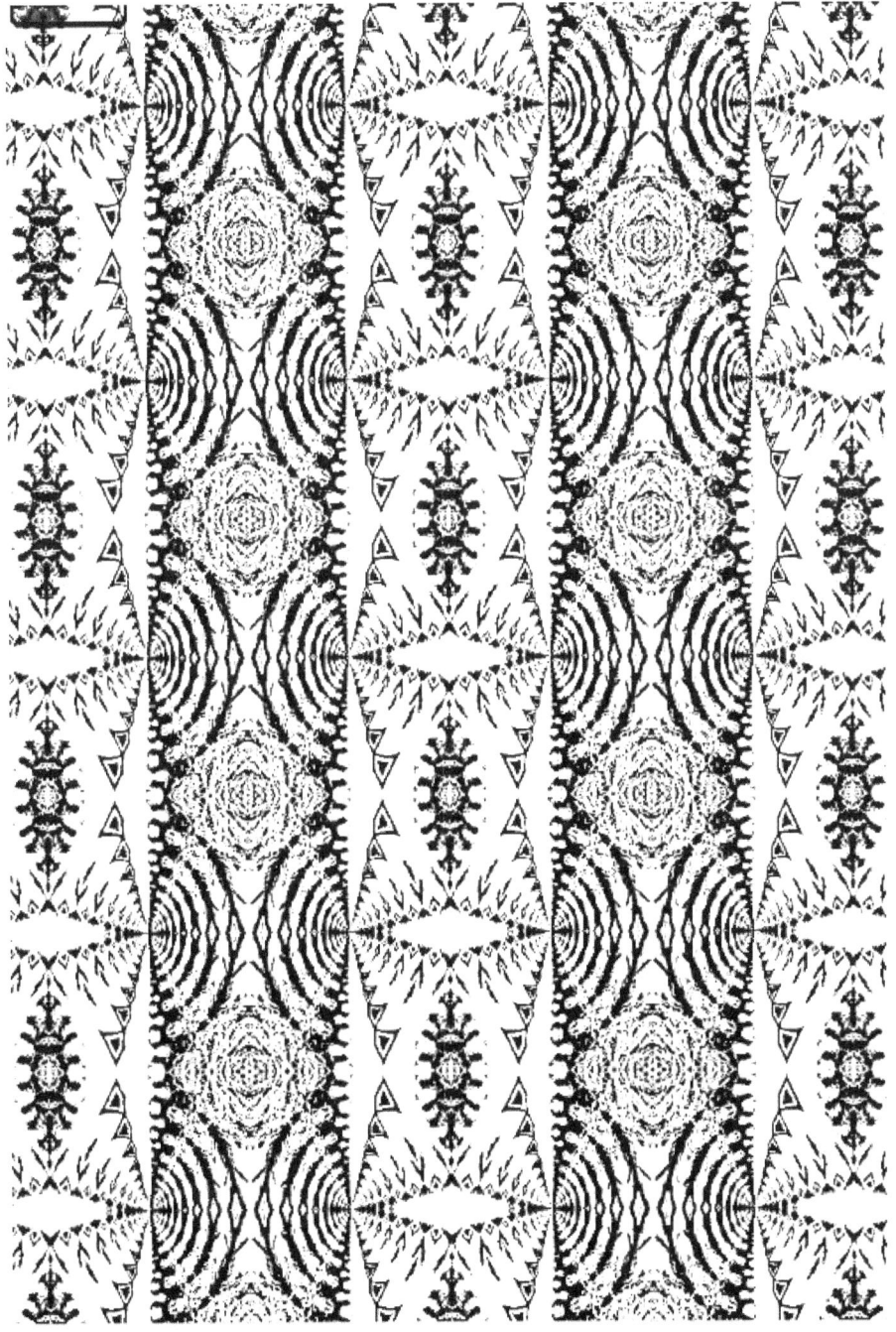

# THINK

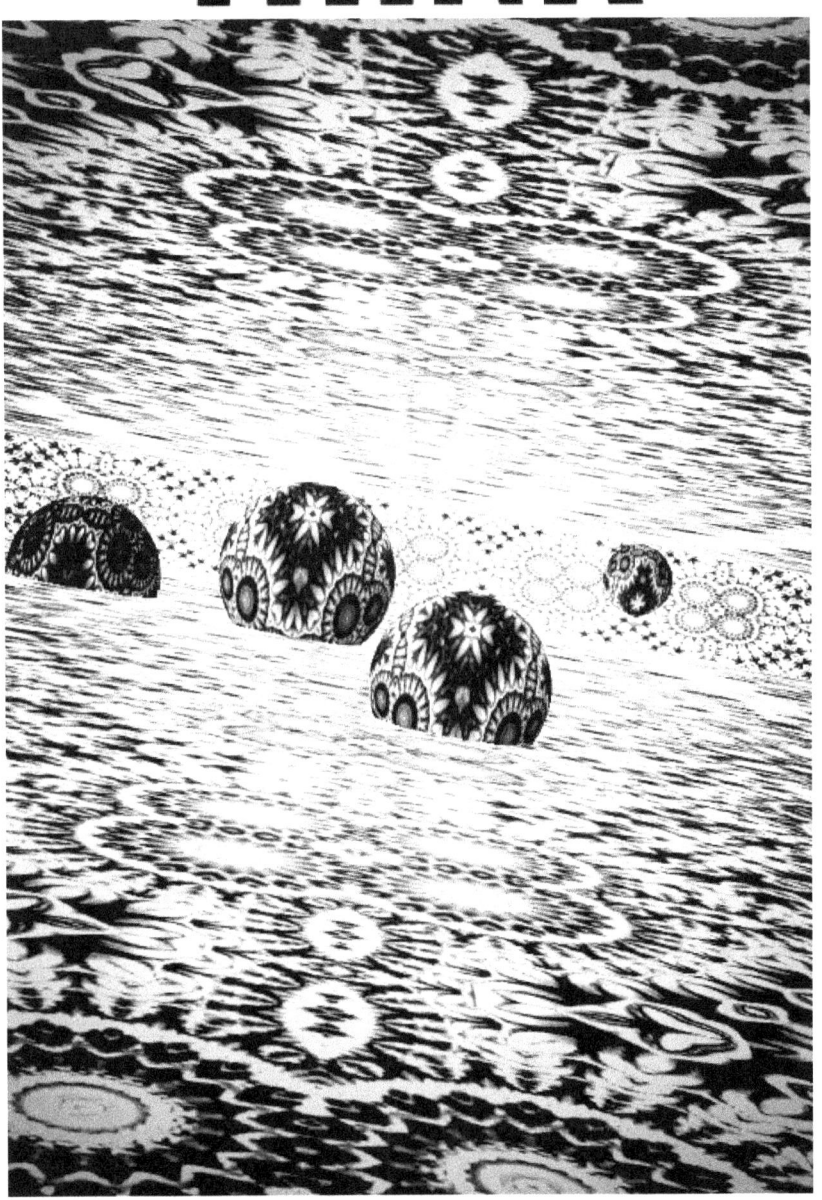

# BIGGER

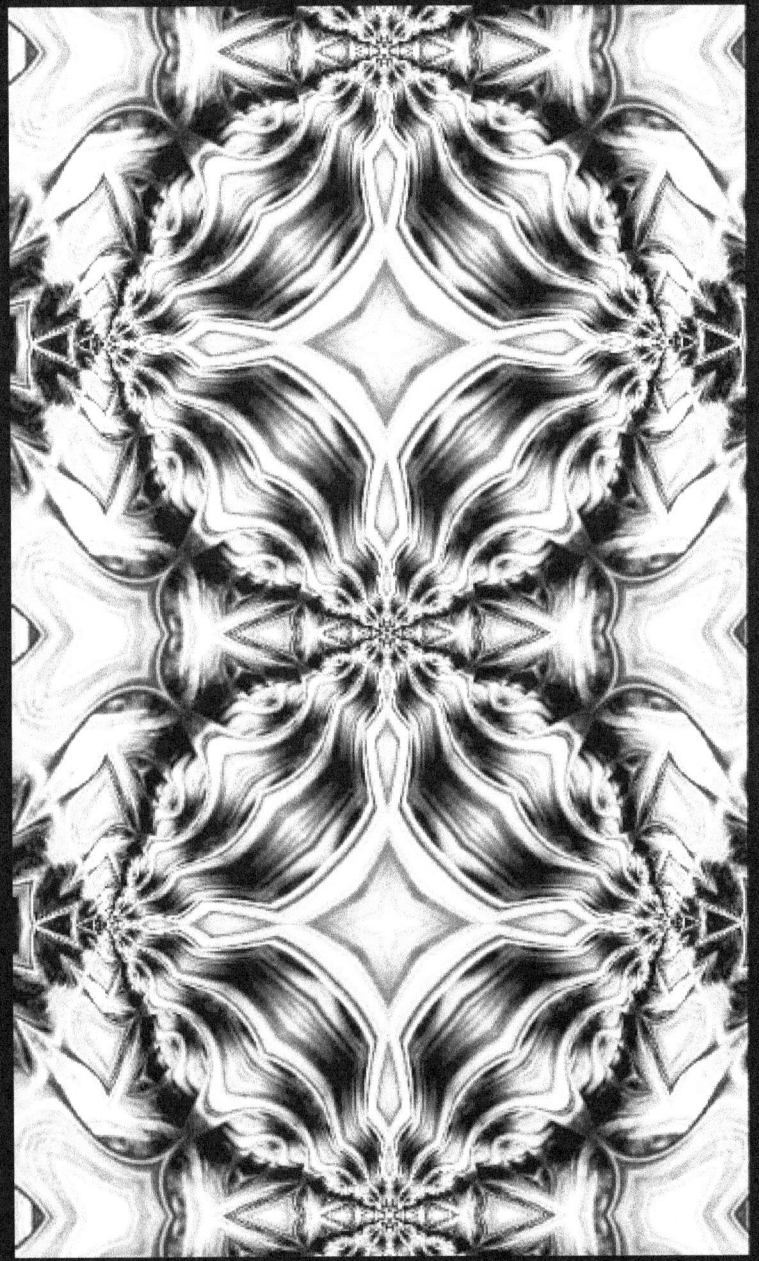

# YOUR SILENCE

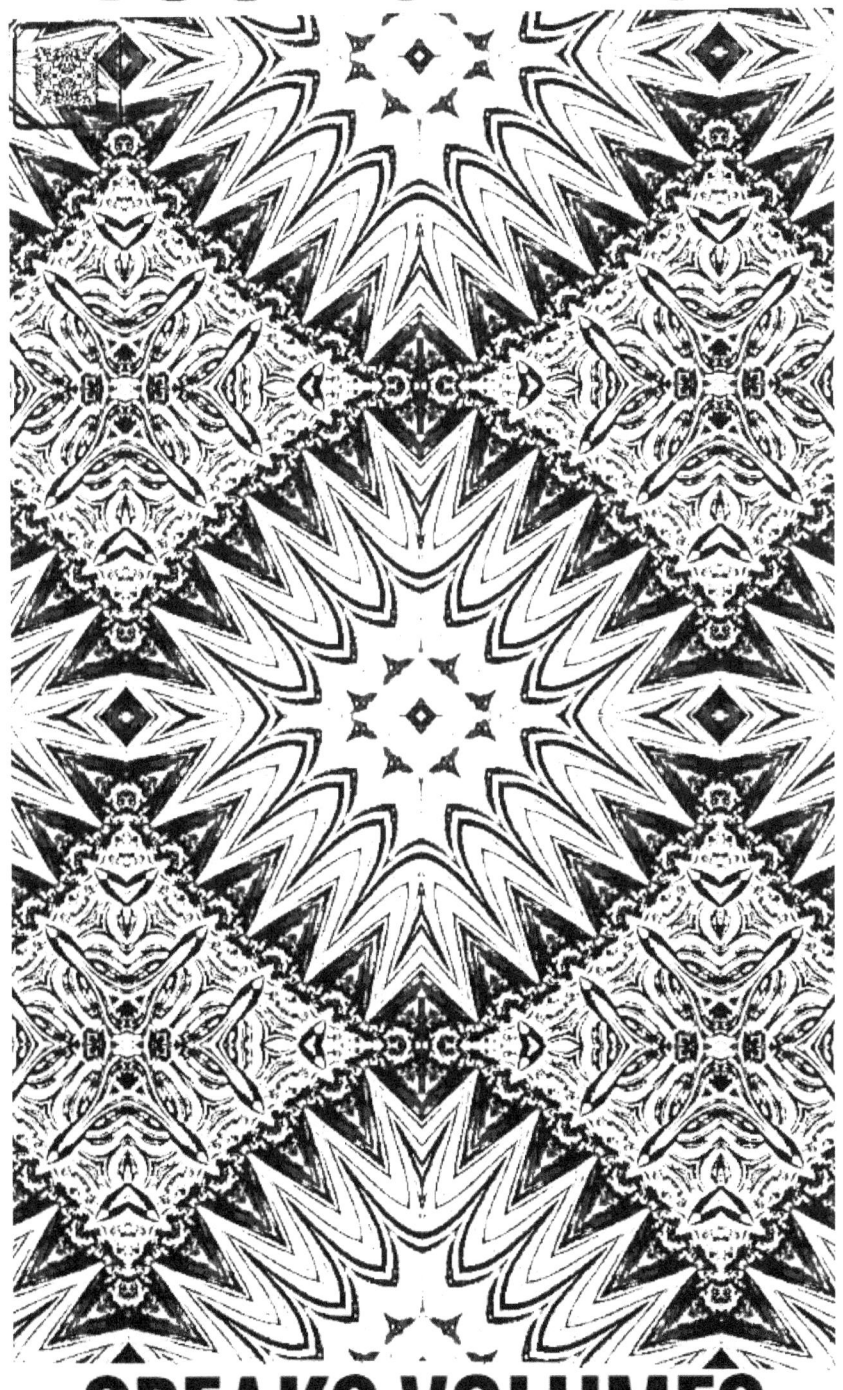

# SPEAKS VOLUMES

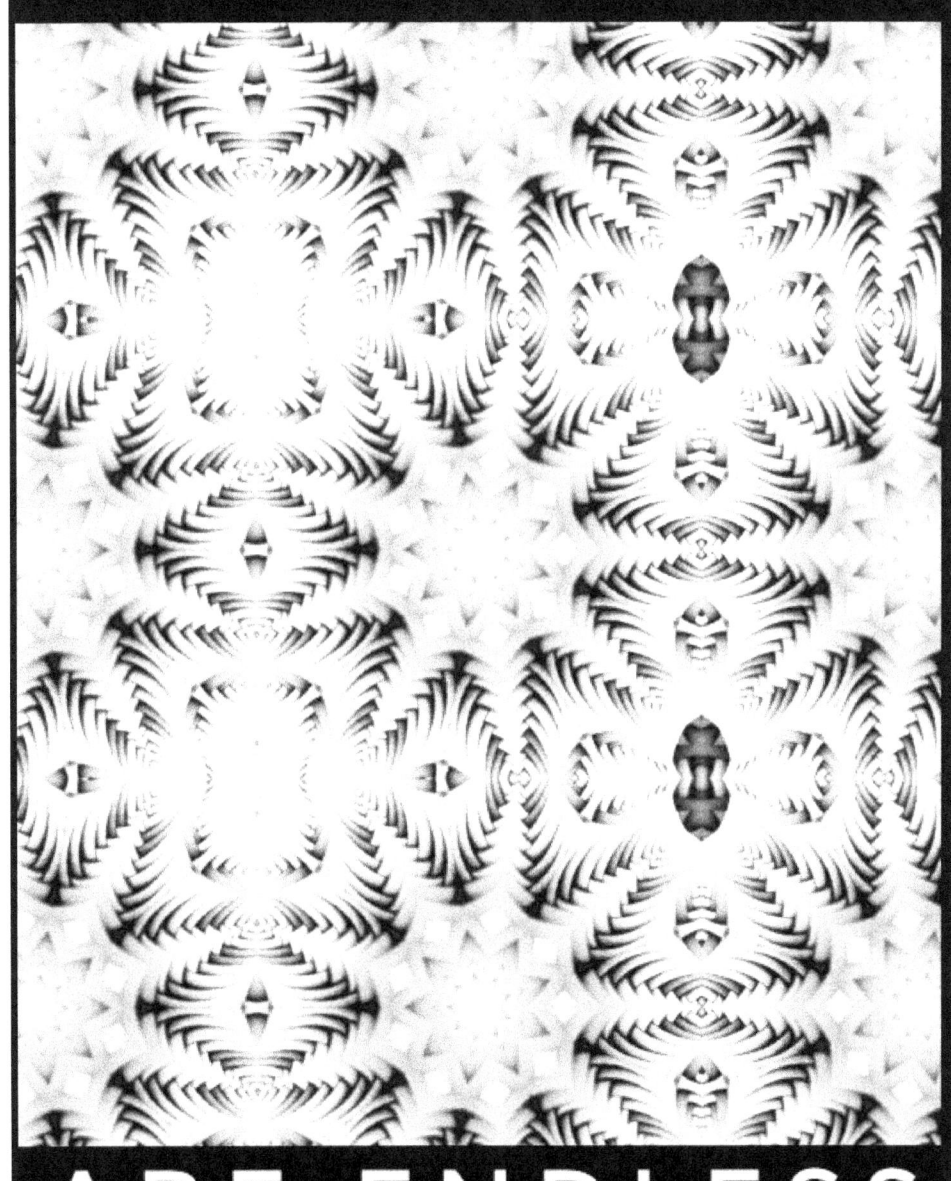

# THINK

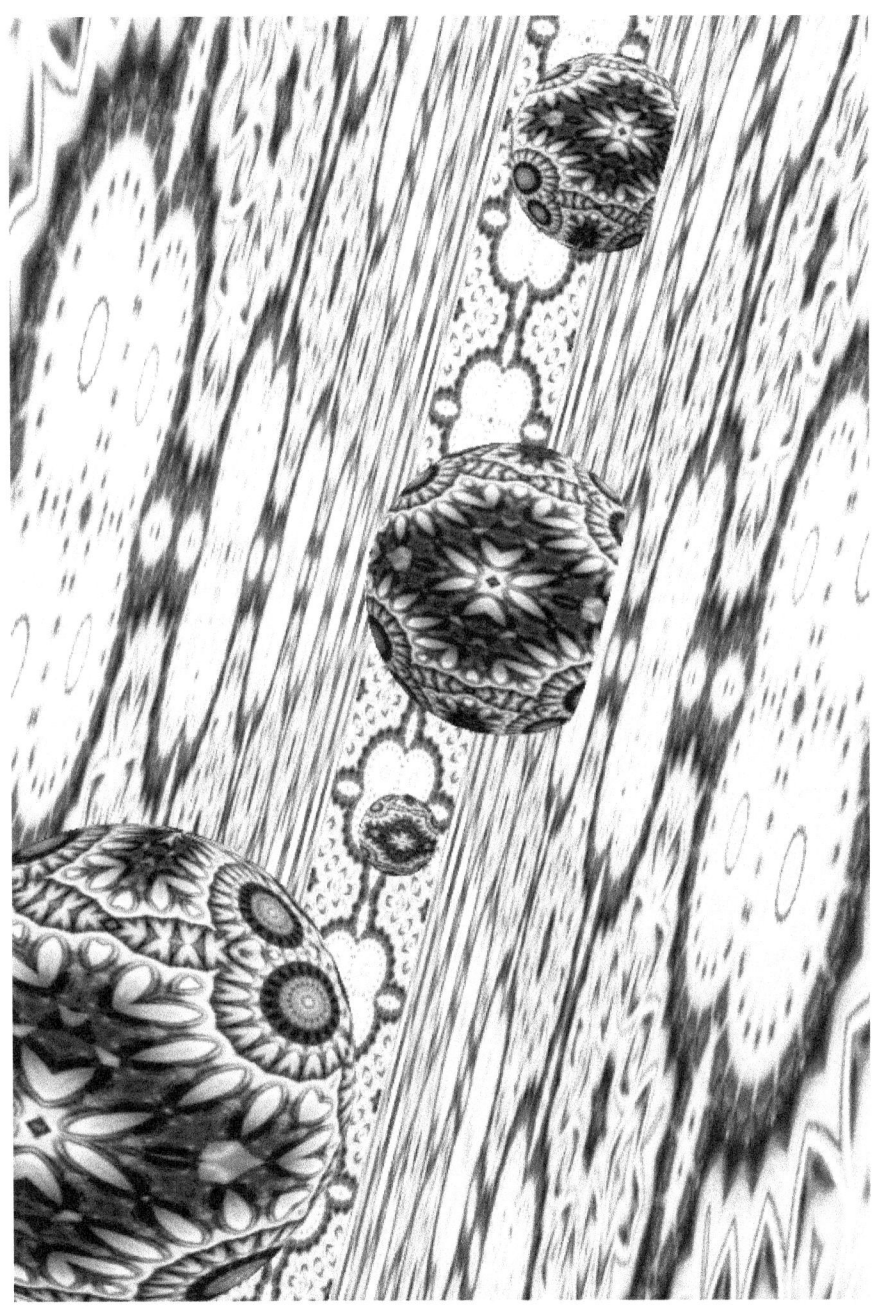

# POSITIVE

# LOOK

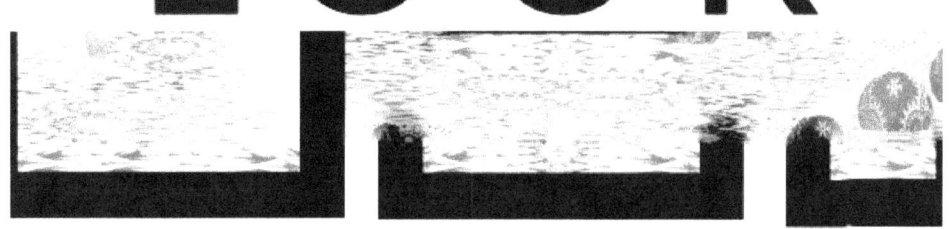

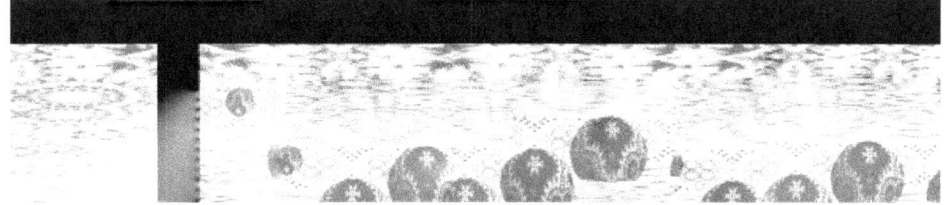

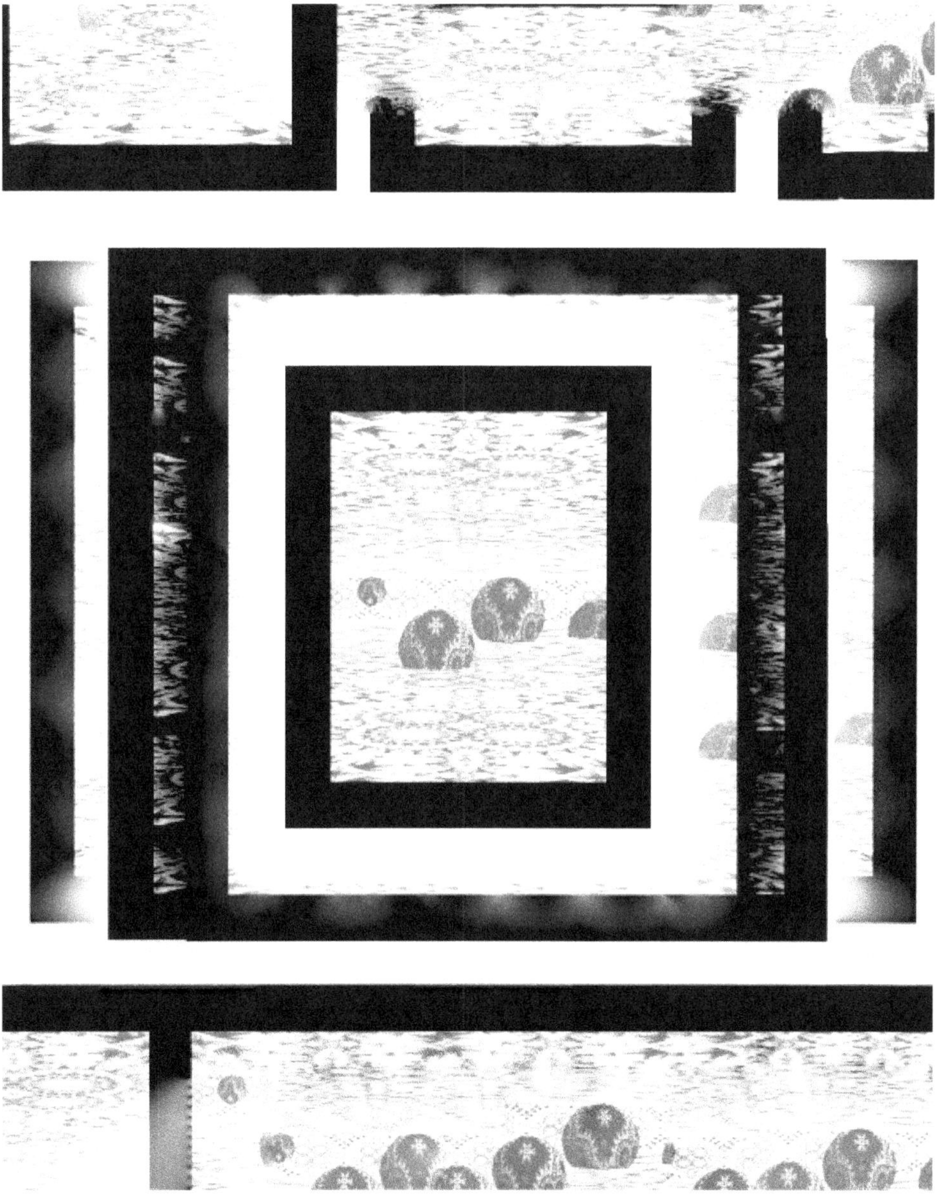

# INSIDE

# YOU ARE

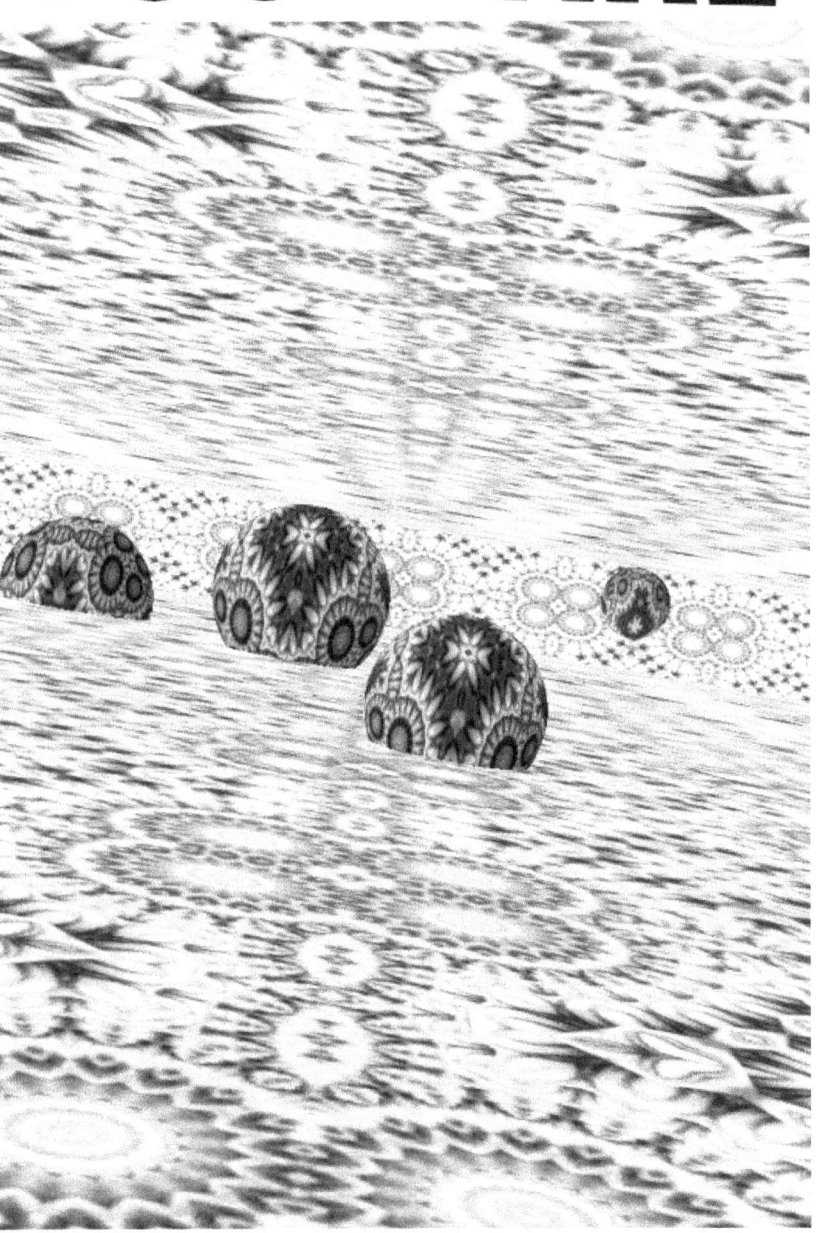

# INFINITY

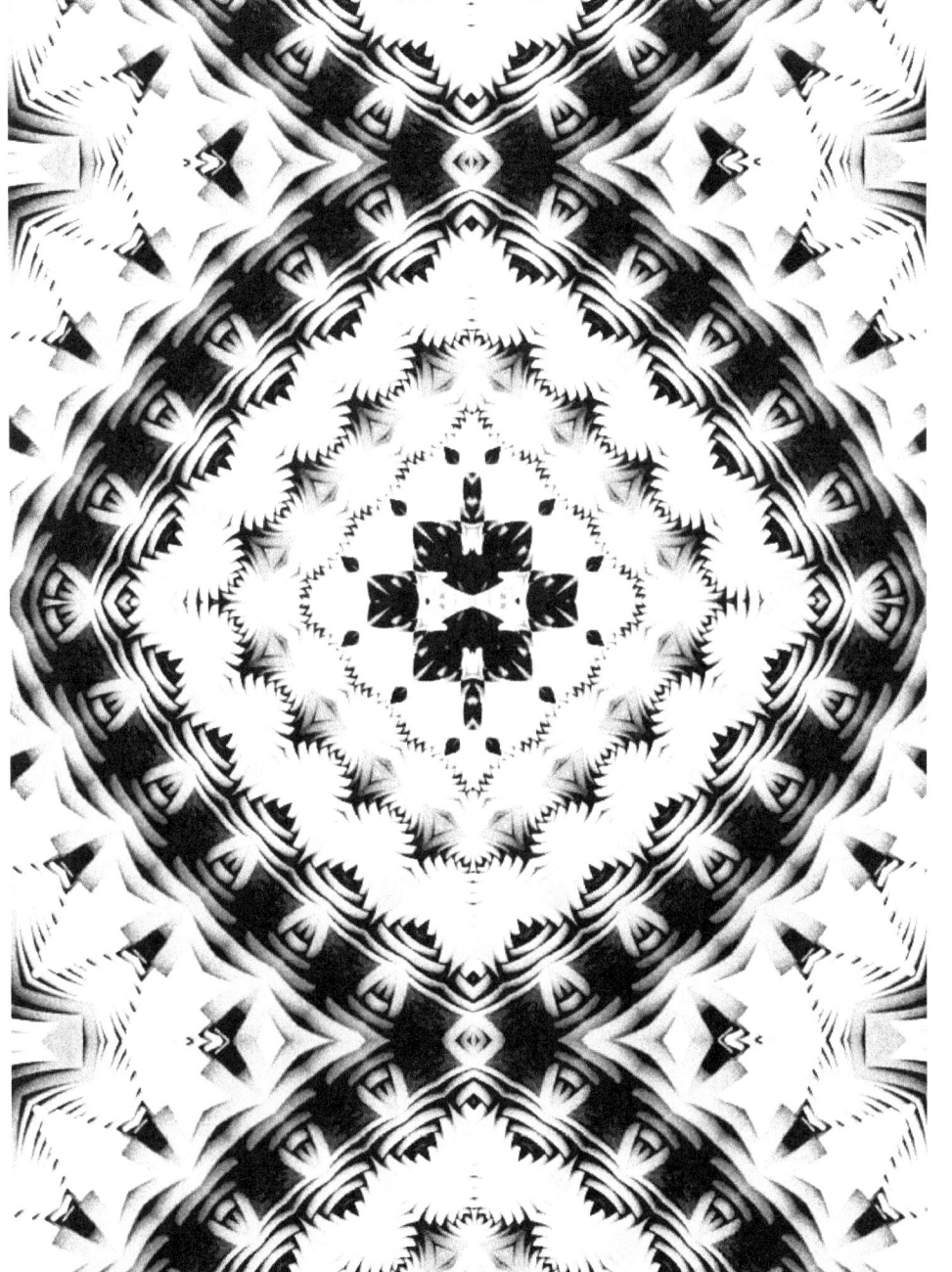

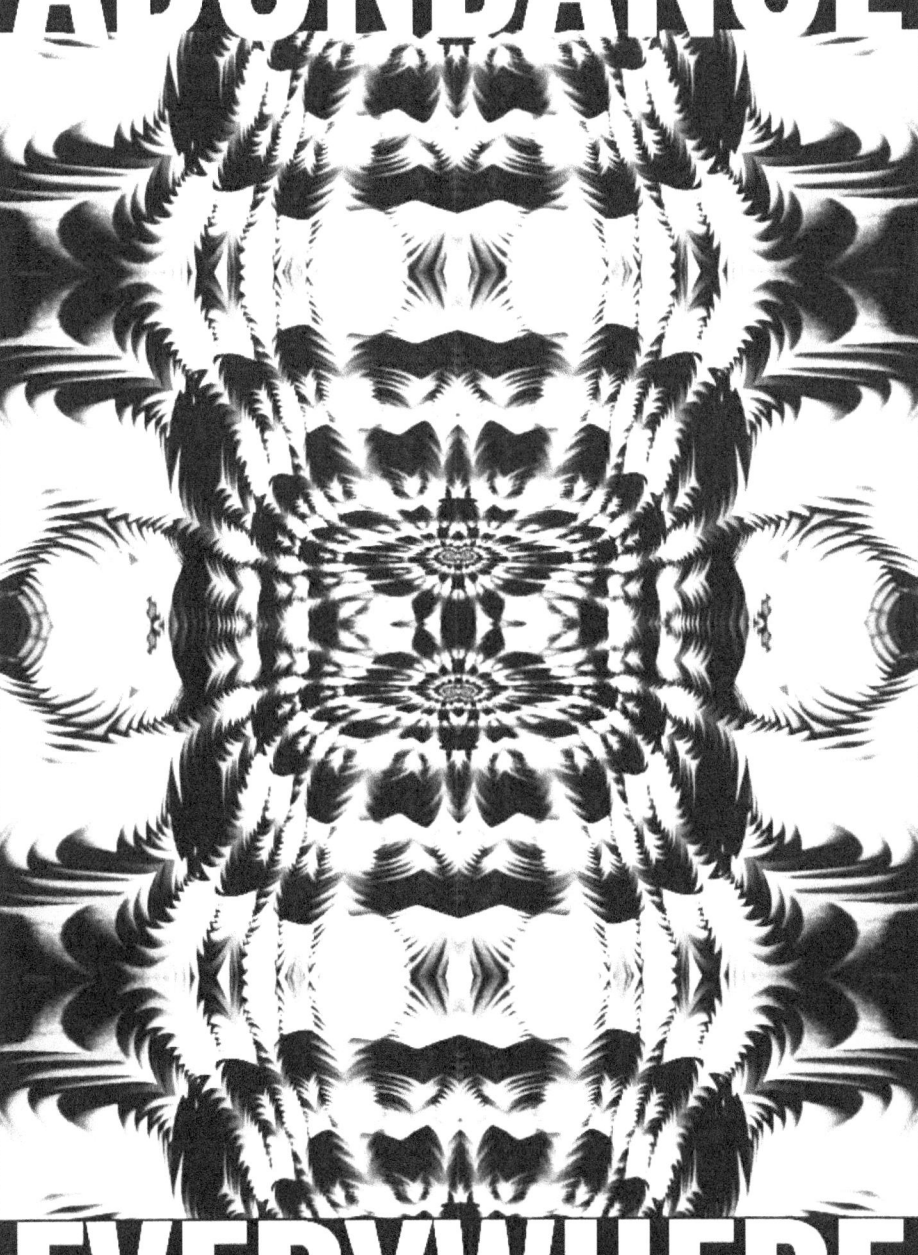

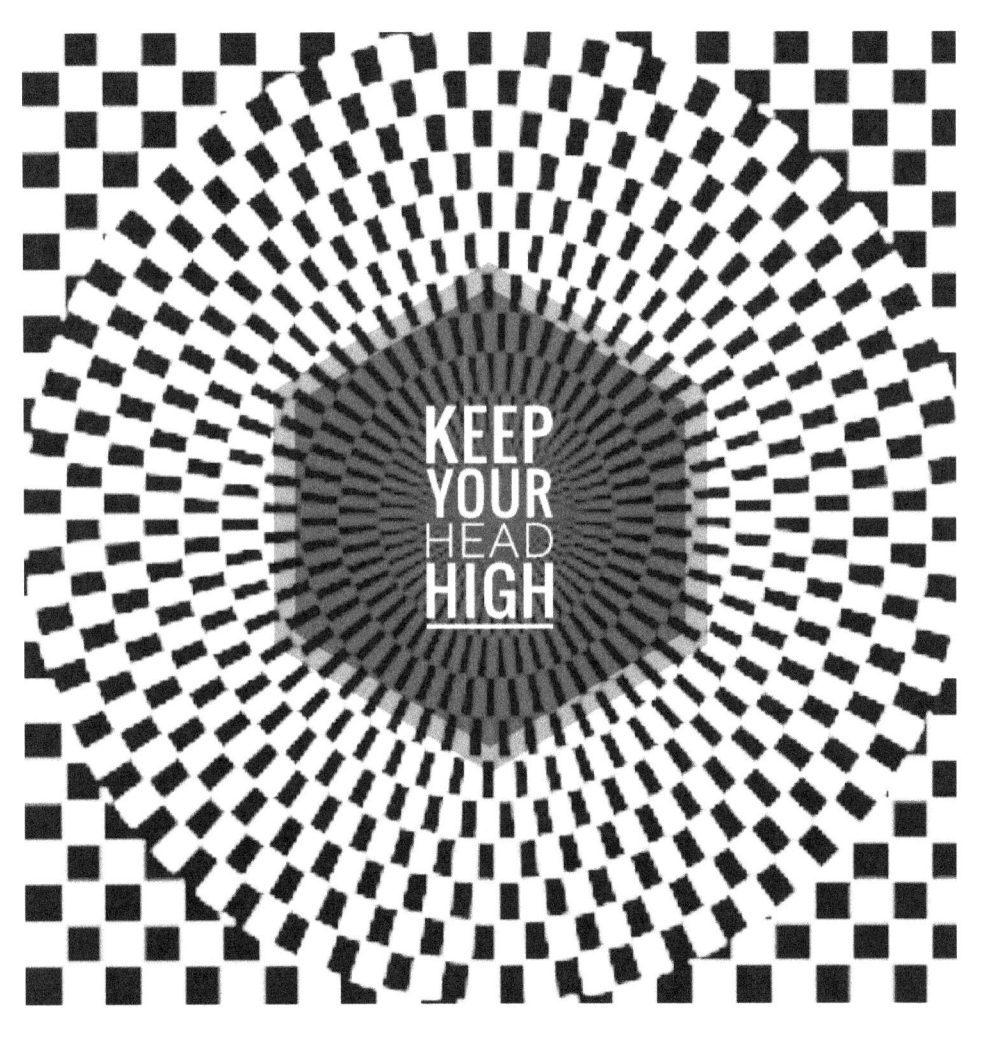

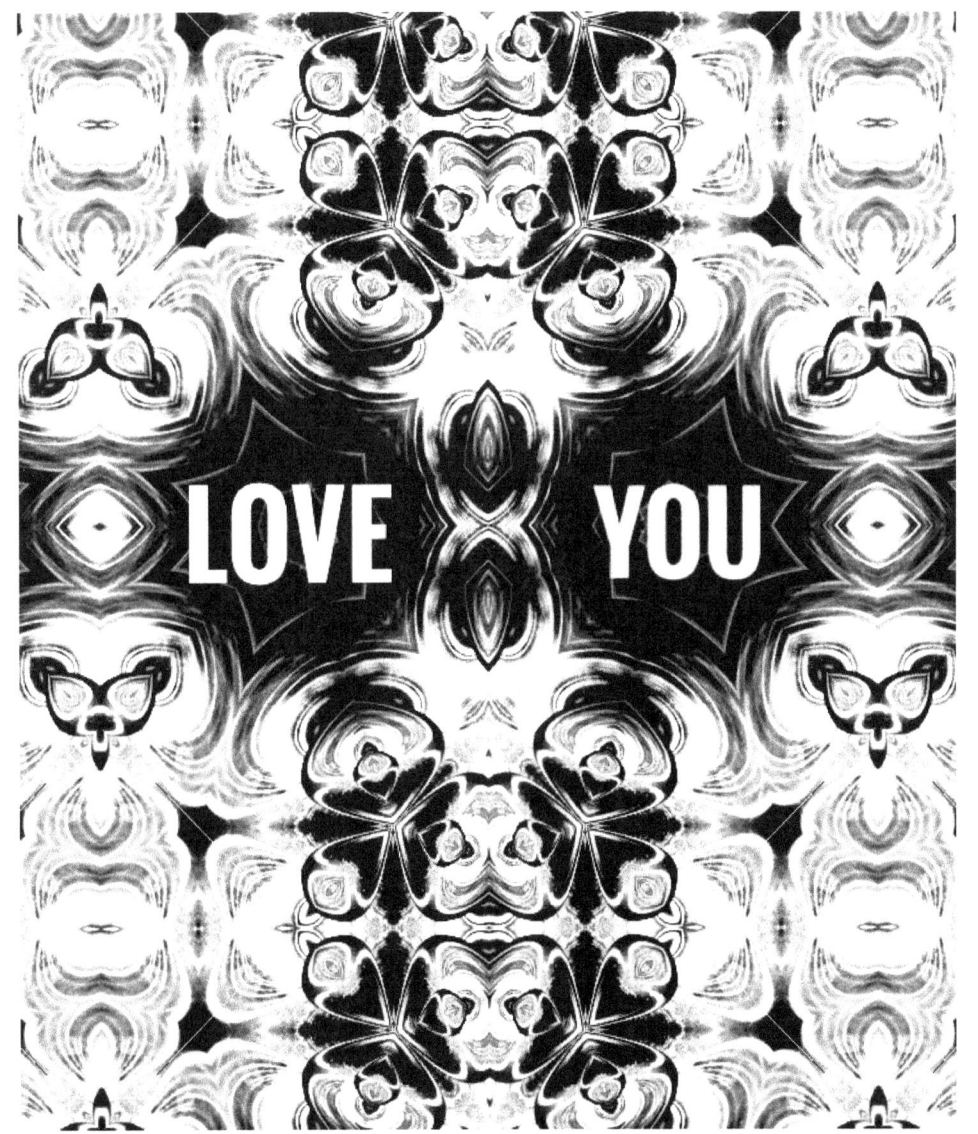

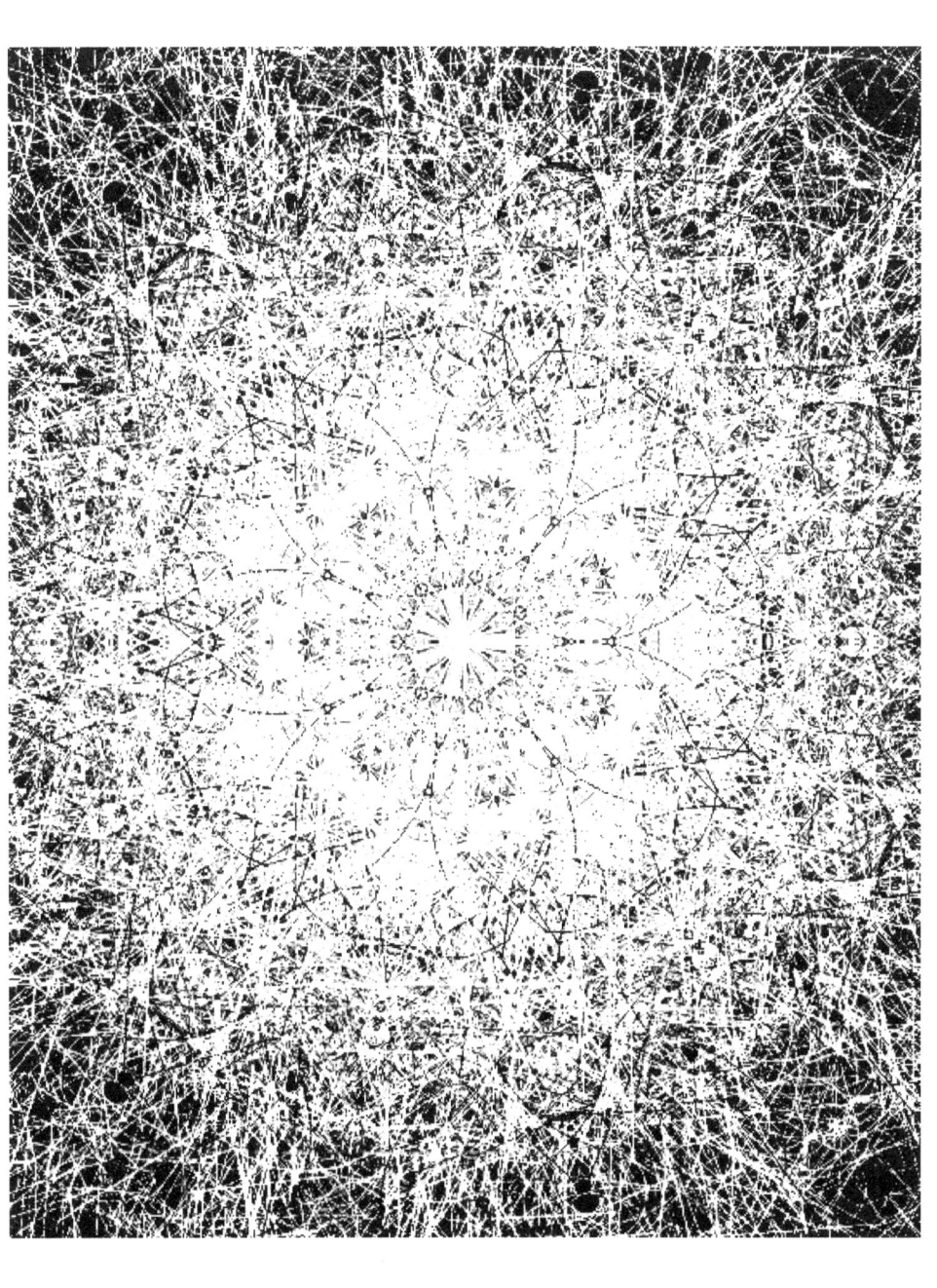

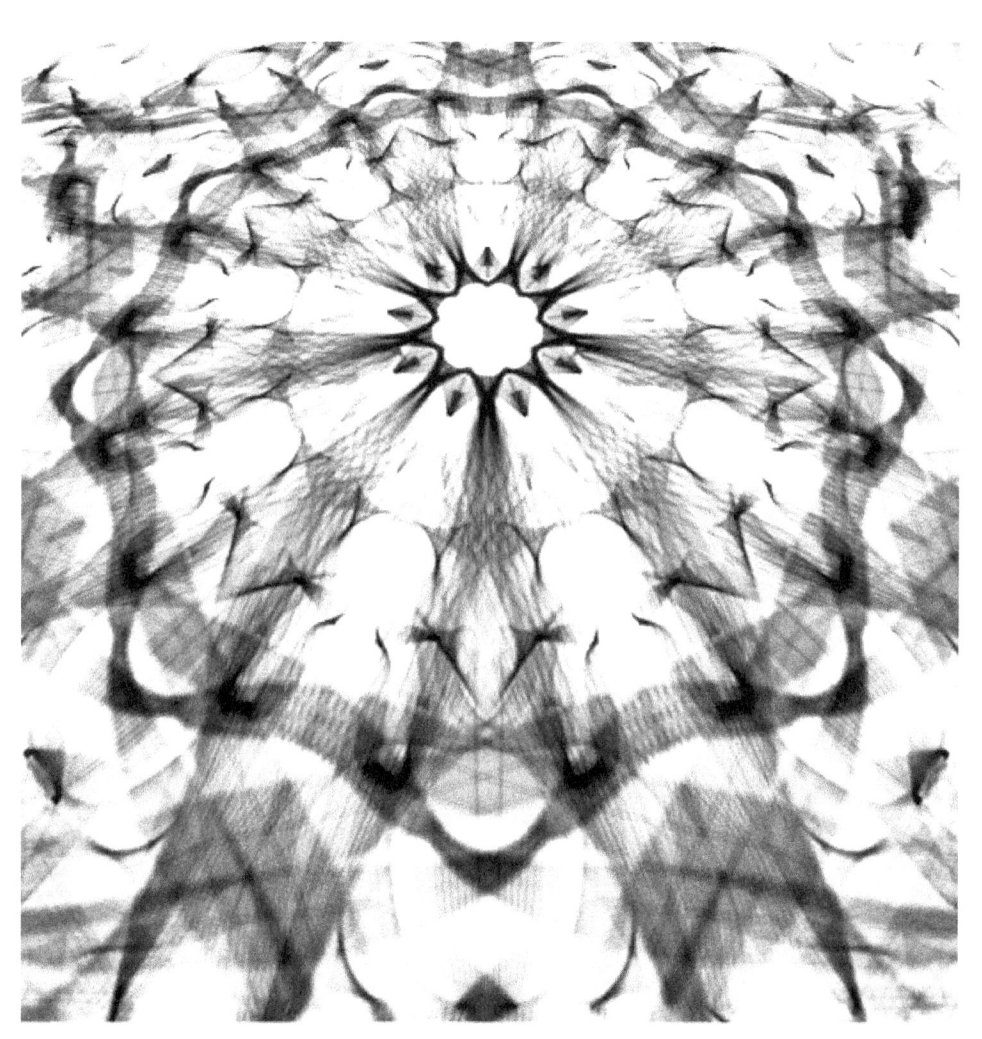

**YOU CAN CHANGE THE WORLD**

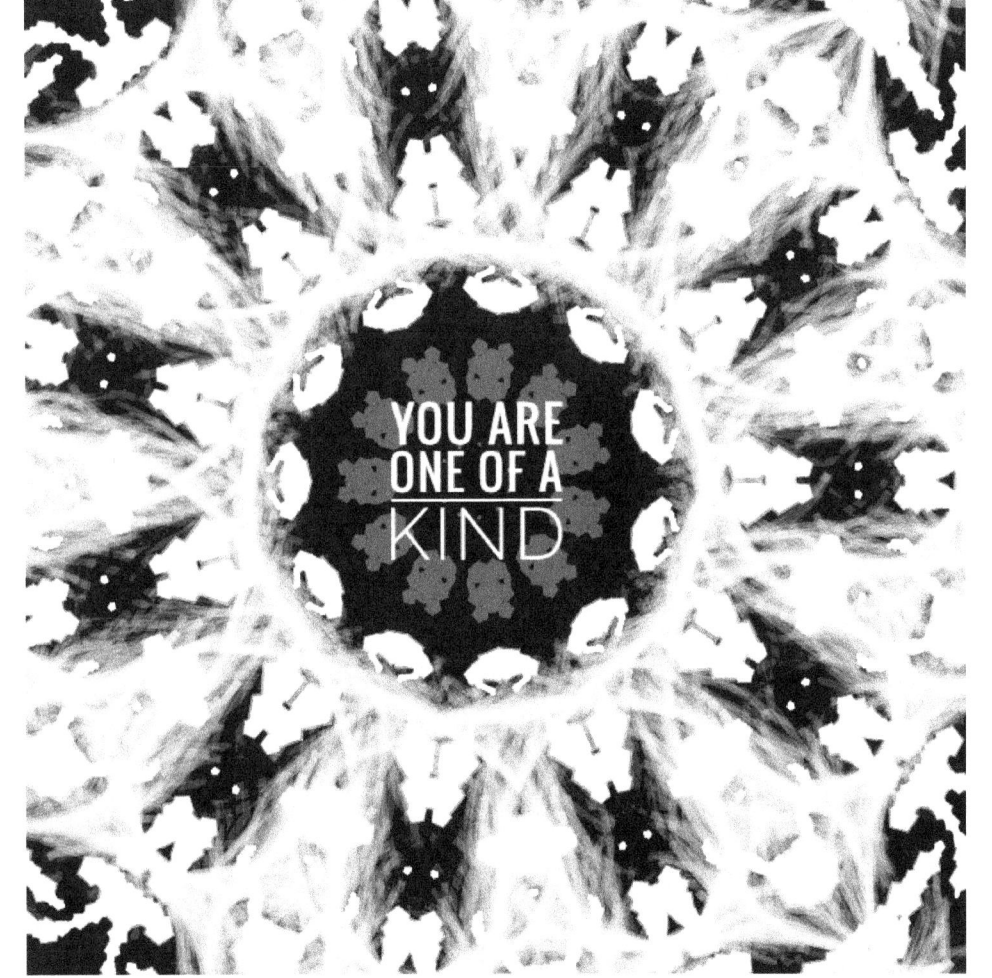

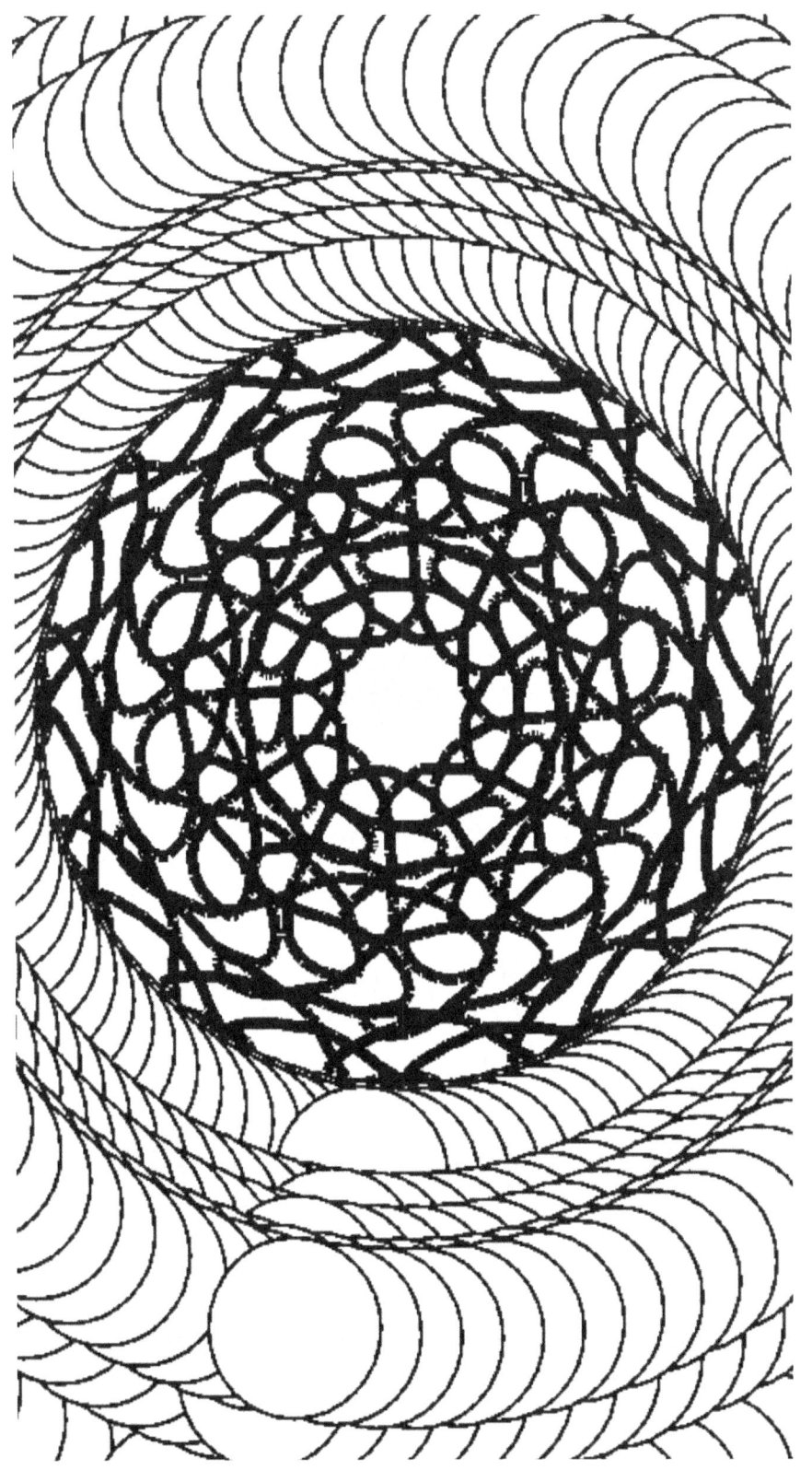

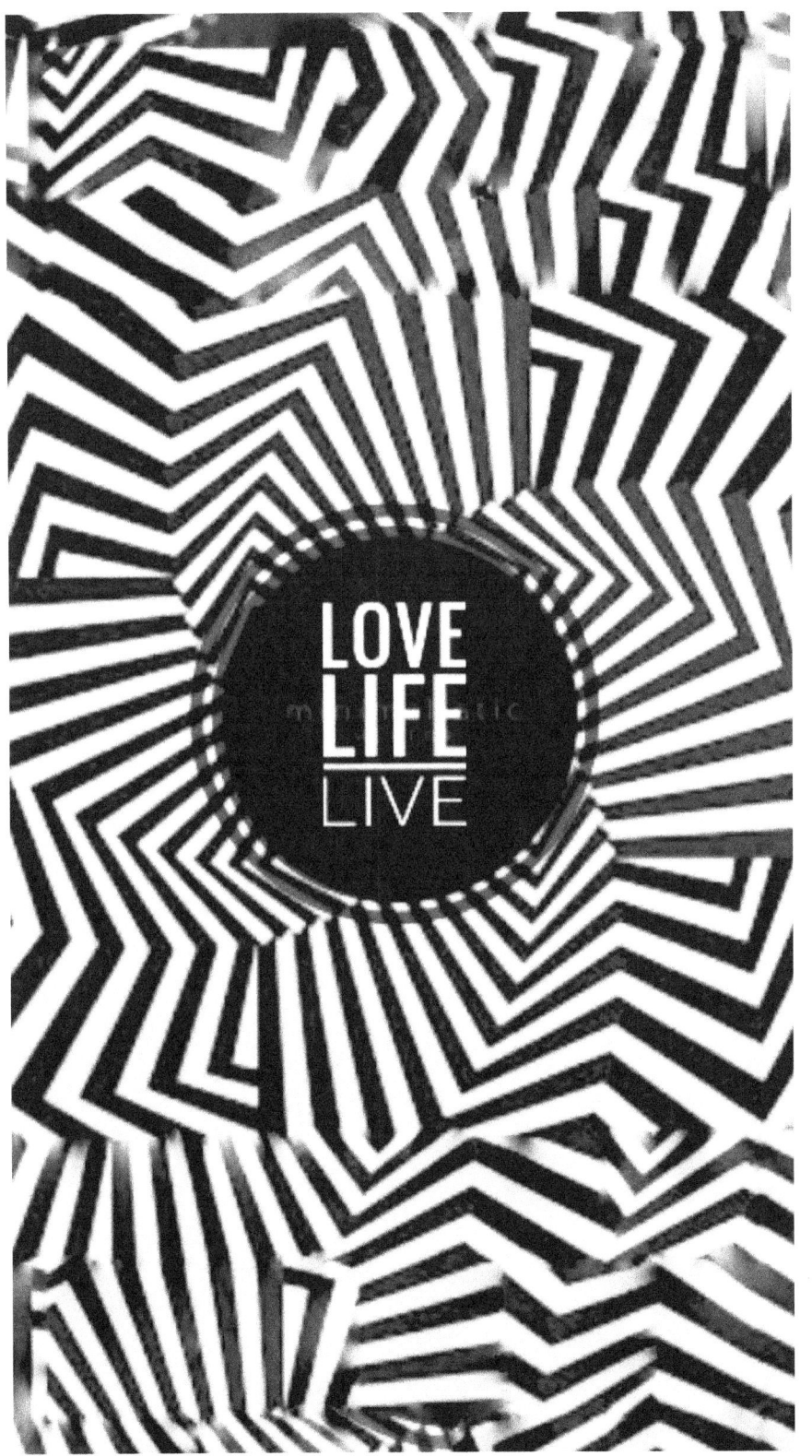

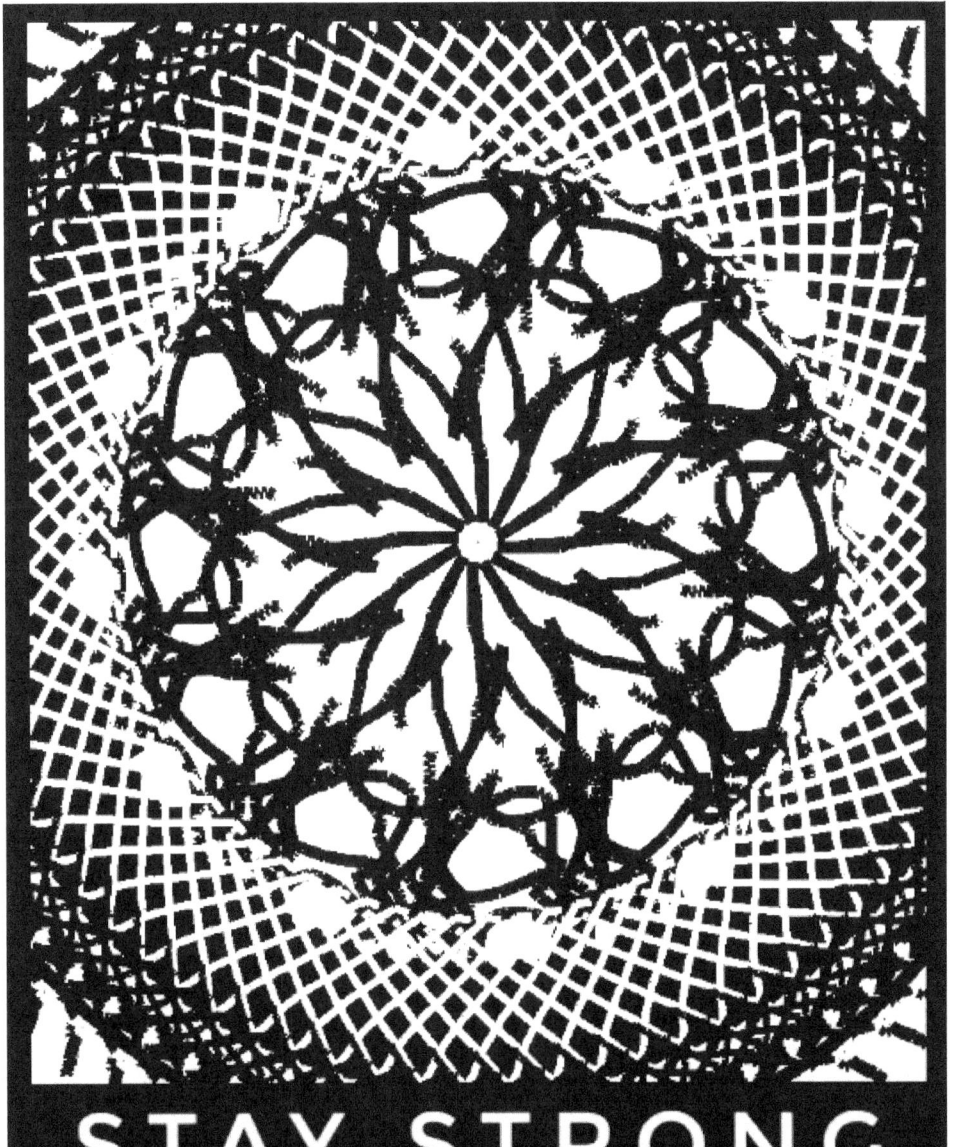

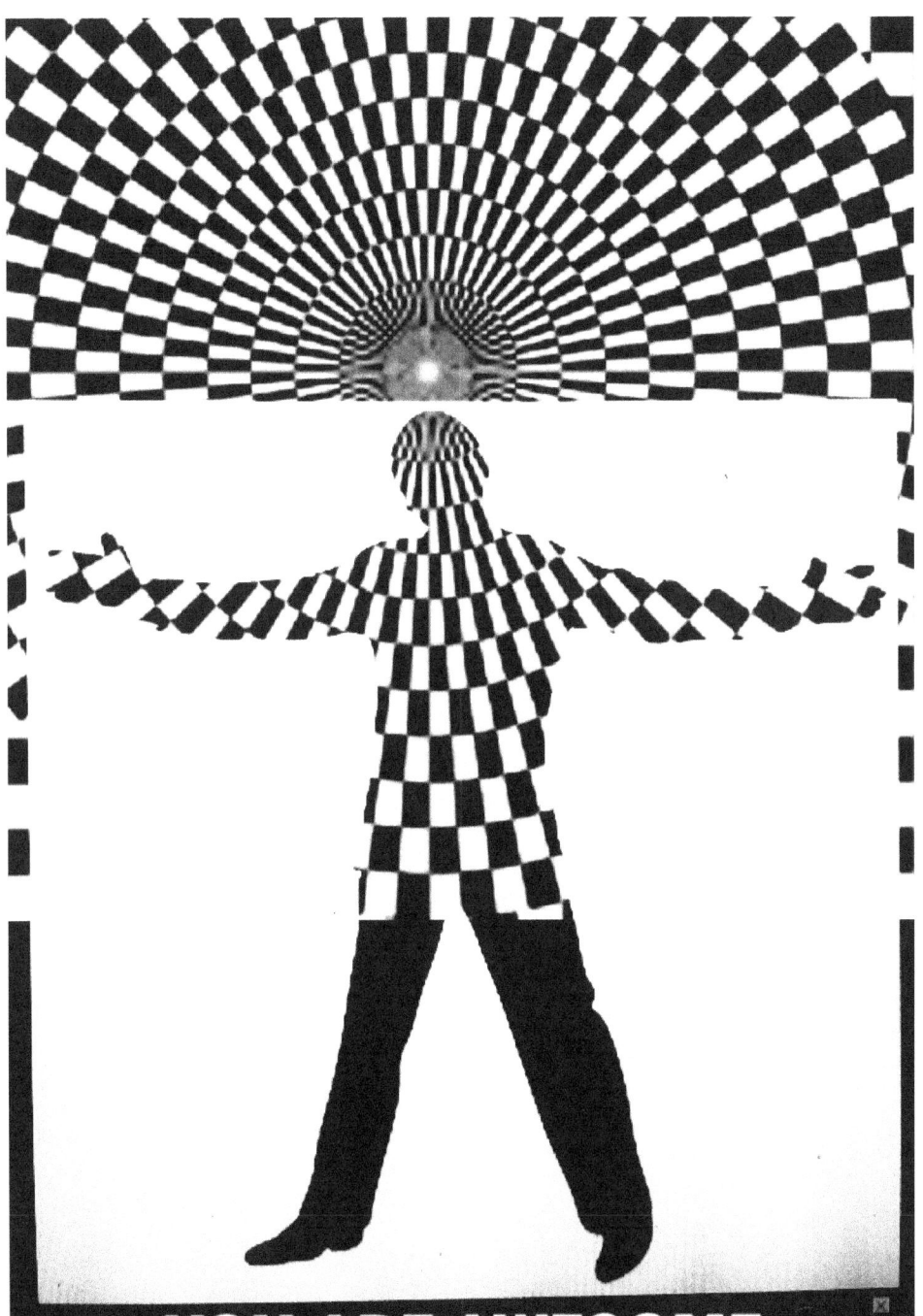

# FORGIVE

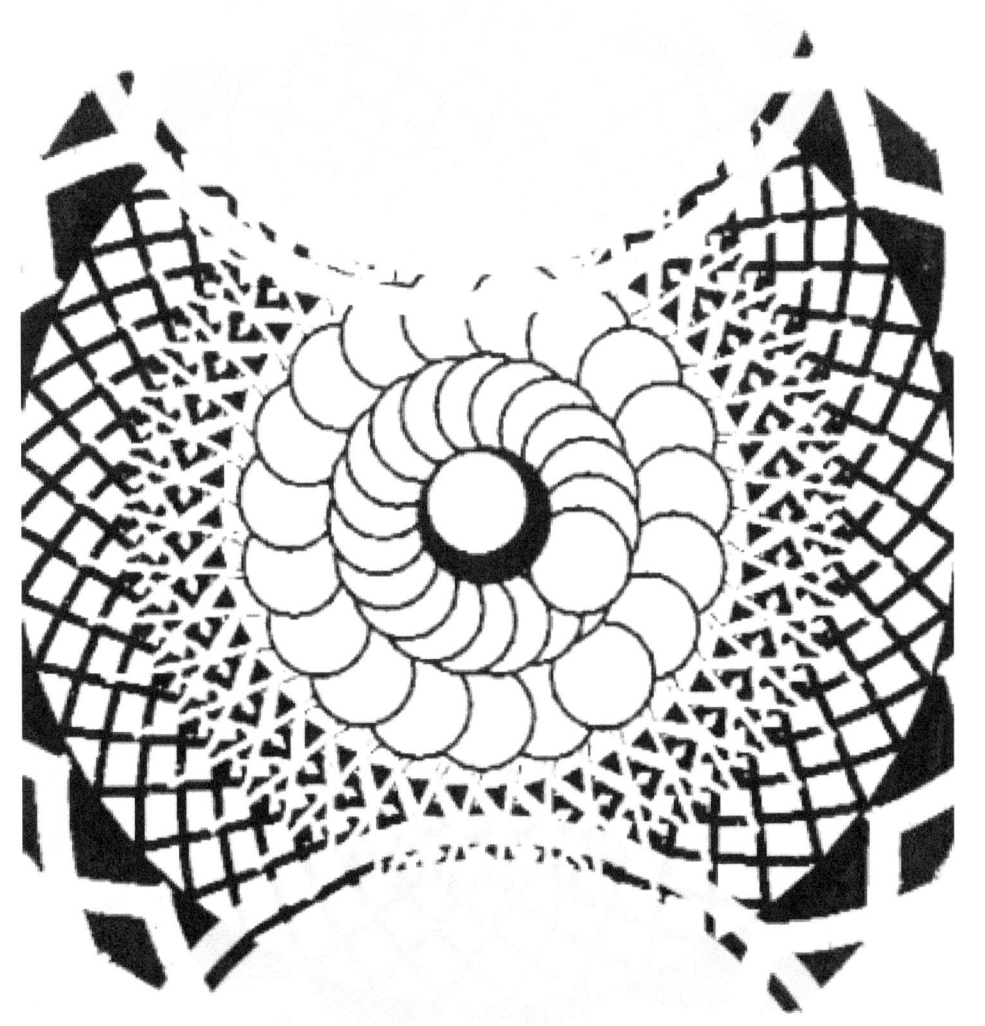

## YOURSELF

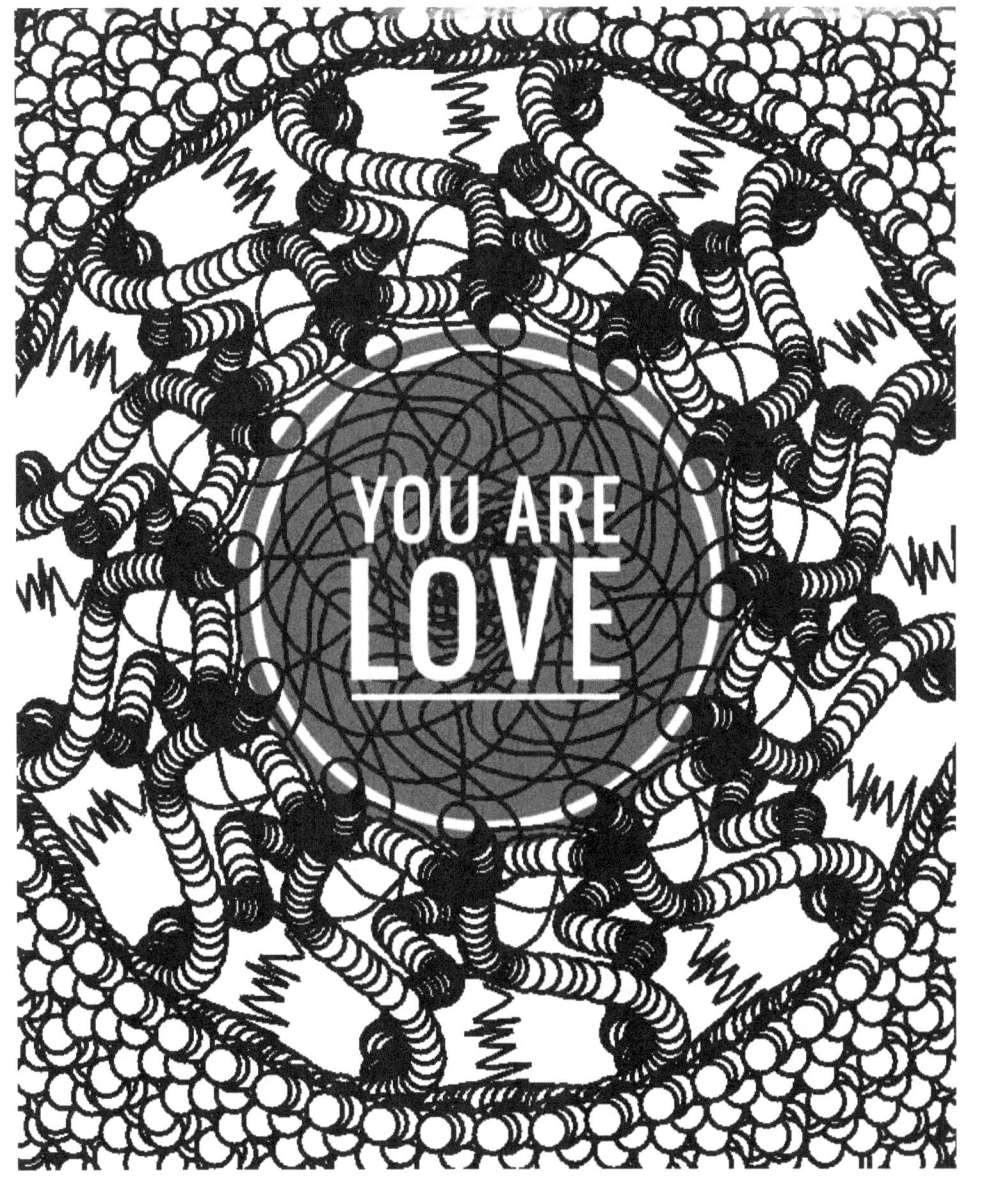

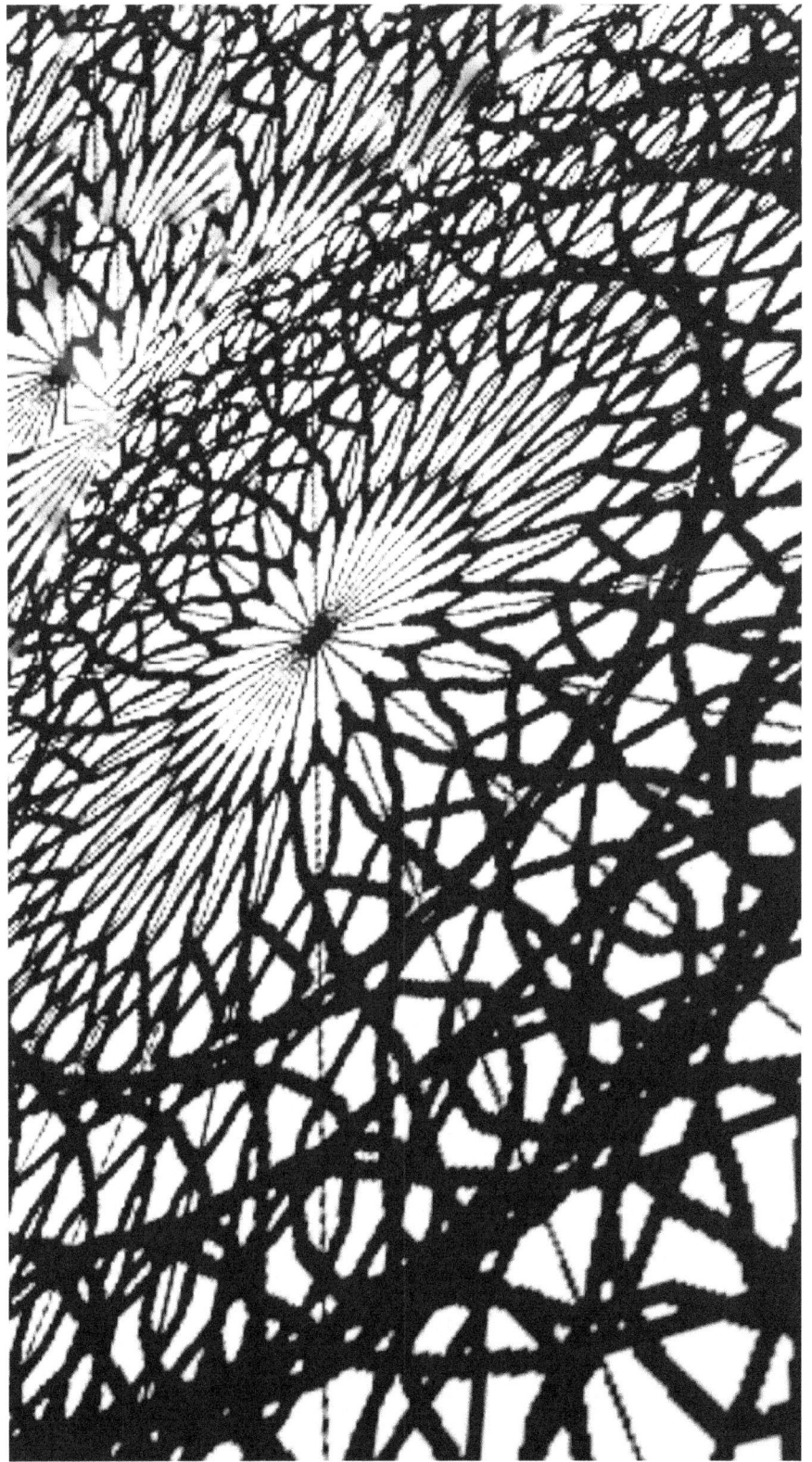